T0266261

MIND & BODY

Published in 2021 by The School of Life
First published in the USA in 2021
930 High Road, London, N12 9RT

Copyright © The School of Life 2021
Design and illustrations by Marcia Mihotich
Typeset by Kerrypress
Printed in Latvia by Livonia

A proportion of this book has appeared online at
www.theschooloflife.com/articles

The School of Life publishes a range of books on essential topics in
psychological and emotional life, including relationships, parenting,
friendship, careers and fulfilment. The aim is always to help us to
understand ourselves better – and thereby to grow calmer, less confused
and more purposeful. Discover our full range of titles, including books
for children, here:
www.theschooloflife.com/books

The School of Life also offers a comprehensive therapy service, which
complements, and draws upon, our published works:
www.theschooloflife.com/therapy

www.theschooloflife.com

ISBN 978-1-912891-46-7

10 9 8 7 6 5 4 3

MIX
Paper | Supporting
responsible forestry
FSC
www.fsc.org   FSC® C002795

MIND & BODY

*Mental Exercises for
Physical Well-being*

*Physical Exercises for
Mental Well-being*

CONTENTS

Introduction: The mind-body problem

One of the most peculiar things about being human is that we exist as both minds and bodies. We are in part miraculous machines hung off collagen and calcium skeletons, irrigated by five litres of watery plasma richly packed with erythrocytes and leukocytes driven along 100,000 miles of blood vessels by a pump that beats 100,000 times a day using power released by the breakdown of potato chips and carrot sticks, buttered toast and lemon pie, all tightly sealed in a one-litre vat filled with a mixture of hydrochloric acid and potassium and sodium chloride.

And yet we are at the same time minds that have memories, imagination, emotions and ideals, unique centres of consciousness that can blend an infinity of fears and insights, excitements and regrets into an unfolding story of identity; minds that can conjure up worlds from spectral blankness, that can classify and order chaos, that can turn mute cries into poetry and agony into arias, that can devise ideas to die or live for and that crave beauty and aspire to wisdom – all within a squelchy 1,400-gram walnut encased in a cavity discreetly silent as to the many universes it contains.

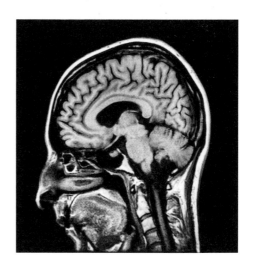

A brain tells us nothing of what it is like to have a mind.

But the two sides of our nature are not only very different; they are also engaged in ongoing and often painful conflict. We wish to be loved and respected for the subtleties of our minds but are in practice more likely to be judged on the shape of our nose and the suppleness of our skin; we seek to impress and reassure with a suggestion of dignity but can't put ourselves beyond the risk of burping or of breaking wind; we long for calm and reason but are fatefully betrayed by debauchery and licentiousness. We hope to honour those we love, do justice to our talents and finish writing our books, but may be ineluctably drawn to nightclubs, too many drinks and the more shameful corners of the internet.

And what is worse, without our conscious selves having any say in the matter, our bodies have catastrophic inclinations to fall apart and die long before we have got the hang of living; before we have tired of seeing springtime or done a fraction of what we suspect we might be capable of.

Gerard van Honthorst,
The Steadfast Philosopher, 1623.
Mind and body are set in opposed
and often inimical directions.

This cluster of tensions, pains and incompatibilities might collectively be referred to as 'the mind-body problem'. Those of a philosophical bent will know that, in academic circles, 'the mind-body problem' means something quite specific. It has been the term used to describe a very particular question identified in the 1640s by the French mathematician and philosopher René Descartes (1596–1650). Descartes wished to know how a purely mental thought could have physical consequences: how, for instance, might a wish to drink a glass of water lead one physically to take a sip? Descartes imagined the material world like a complex set of billiard balls: everything happens in it because one thing pushes another. But a thought doesn't seem to have any material properties: it has no physical weight, so how could it be involved in pushing anything? How could it make something physical move? How could a weightless thought cause the muscles of our fingers to contract? Although no really convincing strategy for answering this question was available until the rise of neuroscience at the end of the 20th century, the question of how thoughts might lead to physical motion seriously troubled only a very small minority. It would therefore be a pity if the resonant phrase 'the mind-body problem' were forever to be attached only to this arcane conundrum, the answer to which no element of human happiness has ever seriously depended upon. It therefore feels fitting to reappropriate and employ the phrase to refer to all the dilemmas thrown up for us by our dual nature as physical bodies on the one hand and as thinking and dreaming souls on the other.

At the core of the mind-body problem thus redefined is the question of whether there might be a way of reducing the strife between the different parts of ourselves. What is the best way to flourish given our dual natures? Can mind and body be constructive companions rather than ill-tempered enemies? Can we learn to accommodate our varied selves with grace? This is the enquiry at the heart of this book, a journey to discover ways of reconciling mind and body in the name of leading more harmonious and less fractured lives.

—

Over the centuries, there have been some unfortunate ways of responding to the tensions between mind and body. The most notable and emblematic of these began in the early 3rd century with the Christian intellectual and saint Origen of Alexandria.

Unknown artist,
Origen, from *Numeros homilia XXVII*, c. 1160.
Origen of Alexandria: the dawn of the mind-body problem.

Origen was an extremely pious man, one of whose earliest wishes was to die as a martyr to Christ. He thought of revealing his faith to the Roman authorities and then awaiting the mandatory death sentence, but after mentioning his ambition to his mother, let himself be persuaded to become an academic instead. He turned out to have great talent in this area, and wrote twenty-five volumes of commentary on the Gospel of St Matthew and 2,000 treatises on biblical hermeneutics.

But despite his devotion to his holy studies, Origen couldn't ignore certain powerful physical attractions that coursed through him. He came to see the body as a prison and argued that we are 'fallen angels' who used to live in heaven but were turned away from God and, as a punishment, had our souls locked up in packets of sinful, suffering flesh. After growing overwhelmed by feelings for one of his biblical students, reputedly the most beautiful nun in Egypt, Origen decided to cut off his penis and testicles in order to avoid

Unknown miniaturist, *Origen Castrating Himself before a Nun*, 14th century, from *Roman de la Rose*, c. 1380.
One way of responding to the mind-body problem: Origen castrating himself rather than submitting to the physical attractions of a nun.

further temptation and make himself 'a eunuch for the kingdom of heaven'. Whether he actually did so is a matter of historical dispute, but Origen's supporters (and the Christian Church more broadly) enthusiastically spread the rumour as proof of exemplary virtue and wisdom, rather than – as others might have proposed – an indication of psychopathology.

Origen's feelings towards his body set the tone for hundreds of years of Christian morality. The body was deemed weak and the realm of the devil; freedom and happiness could only be found by controlling, censoring and, ultimately, destroying this unruly vessel. Under the aegis of Origen's ideas, the faithful in Medieval Europe took to whipping themselves in public squares to demonstrate the intensity of their faith and the purity of their hearts.

Hartmann Schedel, untitled illustration from the *Nuremberg Chronicle*, c. 1493. Flagellants proving their devotion to Christ.

A thousand years after Origen's birth in the 12th century, many of the grandest, most elaborate buildings were decorated with statues that conveyed his ideas about the body. At Chartres, thirty miles south-west of Paris, the doors of the

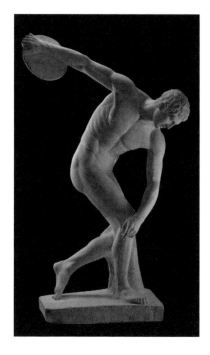

(Above) *The Townley Discobolus*, c. 460–450 BCE;
(Right) Statues of the Royal Portal, Chartres Cathedral, c. 1145–1245. A far cry from the Greeks; the Christian ideal of a tamed and meek body.

cathedral were flanked by static, elongated, ethereal figures, representing the most revered characters of the Christian story. In these saints, the soul had conquered and neutered the body, leaving it limp and docile – a far cry from the muscular, dynamic forms depicted in classical Greek and Roman statues. These saintly beings had no lustful motions and no recognisable muscular arrangement. They were not about to head to the ale house, wolf down a pie, flirt with a neighbour or throw a discus beyond a line of cypress trees.

This physical blankness wasn't what medieval people thought they could achieve themselves. They were horribly conscious of their own earthy and lustful tendencies. What the statues signalled was how they thought they could be if only they could control their wayward sacks of flesh.

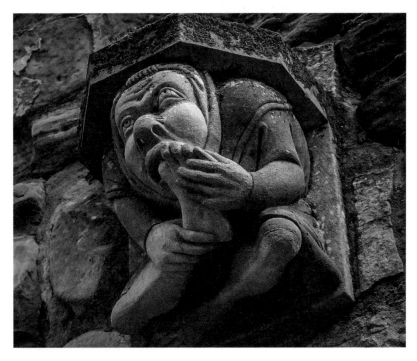

Medieval gargoyle,
Rufford Abbey, c. 1147–1170.
Medieval reality.

Perhaps Origen's most consequential conviction was his argument that Jesus (the person he most admired) must himself have been ugly and lacking in physical allure, for only then could his followers have been convinced by his philosophy rather than his physique. Origen proposed that God would have made him look as repulsive as possible in order to guarantee that our love for him would be sincere. This sounds like a bizarre point of theological controversy. In fact, it was an attitude that shaped the mentality of half the planet for a dominant share of human history. Even today, we find it hard to imagine that a thoughtful and profound soul could exist in an alluring physical envelope, and might instinctively doubt an intellectual who looked as though they might be able to moonlight as a model.

Without any of Origen's religious baggage, we still have moods in which we consider our bodies to be the source of an overwhelming share of our troubles, and might happily dispose of them if we could. The English novelist Kingsley Amis (1922–1995), towards the end of a long life, looking back over decades of sexual complications and regrettable drunken evenings, quipped of having a body: 'for fifty years, it was like being chained to an idiot'.

—

There is another, radically different approach: to assume that the body is an uncomplicated friend that we can celebrate and enjoy without wariness or difficulty, merely by deciding to relax our muscles and breathe a little more deeply. This can be the impression given off by certain health clubs, sports enthusiasts, healers and sex-positive evangelists who may unwittingly imply that 2,000 years of shame and suspicion around the body might have been an unfortunate accident, with no profound roots in human nature, and require nothing more to shake off than a momentary effort of the will, a refreshing trip to the sports centre or the right sort of scented candle and body oil.

The novelist Kingsley Amis, tightly chained to his 'idiot'.

But such optimism doesn't feel true to our natures either. We don't have to be tempted by castration to know that our bodies can be tricky entities to live around, that shame is real, that conflicting impulses have their costs and that sex is always at risk of sitting somewhat bizarrely alongside other things we care about. The solution to the mind-body problem is neither to let the mind win, nor to give the advantage wholly to the body; it's to recognise that there are problems and to try to find the most elegant and imaginative ways to assuage them.

Part of the solution lies in a word we're used to thinking of in quite limited terms: exercise. Nowadays, when we think of exercise, we imagine something with a distinctly bodily end in view: we pull on ropes, lift up dumb-bells, push on rowing machines and jog around tracks – all in order, we hope, to get the body into optimal condition.

But there might be forms of exercise with greater ambitions; exercises in which we prompt the mind to remember its kinship with the body and, at the same time, ask the body to assist the mind in entering its most positive states. In other words, there could be varieties of exercise that are specifically designed for psychocorporeal goals that bridge the mind-body divide.

One of the earliest and still most recognised examples of such exercise is to be found in the ancient Indian practice of yoga.

Buddha statue, Sukhothai Historical Park, c. 1292–1347.
A representation of the Buddha in a typical lotus position.

In innumerable temples, Buddha is presented in the lotus position, with each foot crossed over and resting on the opposite thigh. In a literal sense, the lotus position belongs to the realm of physical exercise alone, and in the West it has often been thought of in such limited terms, as just something else to try alongside kettlebells or boxing gloves. But within the Buddhist tradition, the point of adopting particular poses is explicitly spiritual: yoga positions are meant to help us untether ourselves from our egos, renounce vain desires and understand our connections to the cosmos and eternity. Yoga postures were not primarily developed to relax our muscles or elongate our ligaments (though such subsidiary gains are not to be shunned), but to induce our minds to more readily adopt a range of 'higher' states revered by Buddhist thought. The purpose of exercise was to use physical means to induce mental ends.

No one could accuse Buddhism of skating superficially over its exercise regime. The *Yogācārabhūmi-Śāstra*, a 4th-century encyclopaedic text focused on North Indian Mahāyāna Buddhist yoga, is made up of fourteen volumes that take the reader through seventeen levels of enlightenment available to the committed practitioner. Nevertheless, one might argue that classical Asian yoga, for all its profundity, still operates with a relatively limited set of objectives – the progress of the soul towards liberation in the state of nirvana – which do not exhaust the range of options for other kinds of exercise that might be pursued with psychological ends in mind.

Guided by, but not restricted to, the example set by yoga, we could imagine greatly extending our ideas of what physical exercise might henceforth be. There could be exercise not just to help us with Buddhist spiritual detachment, but also – for example – to help us gain confidence, reconnect with friends, accept our imperfections or better appreciate the majesty of the natural world.

This book is structured around six mind-and-body-centred challenges that we tend to face in our lives, in response to which we lay out a menu of exercises. Some take very little time and effort and others require greater commitment, but all of them can edge us towards moods that will best help us flourish. Rather than lamenting the mind-body problem or denying that such a thing exists, we offer a programme of activities to nudge both mind and body to thrive in intelligent harmony.

SOCIABILITY

Introduction

However many friends we might have and however busy our lives, most of us are still often at risk of feeling lonely. It can be hard to feel genuinely accepted and understood, or to connect sincerely with other people, even if we know that deep down they care for us and we for them.

We go to enormous efforts to engineer social occasions where we hope to drop our guard, reveal our vulnerabilities and share our more playful and intimate sides, and yet we can find that inhibition and tradition pull us away from the warmth and sympathy we crave. At the end of many a party, we say farewell to our guests knowing that there was so much more that might have been divulged or created together, but we remain unsure as to what we could have discussed or how we could have drawn out the more tender and profound aspects of one another.

To help us over our isolation, we have designed a range of initially artificial-sounding rituals that nevertheless have a power to liberate the more spontaneous part of ourselves and to be the vehicles for us to express the kindness, spirit of fun and curiosity we deep down possess in abundance. We present seven 'sociability exercises'.

(i) The ecstatic dance

One of the strangest but most intriguing and redemptive things that humans get up to, in almost every culture, is occasionally to gather in large groups, bathe in the rhythmic sounds of drums and flutes, organs and guitars, chants and cries, and move their arms and legs about in complicated and frenzied ways, losing themselves in dance.

Dancing has a claim to be considered among the most essential and salutary activities we ever partake in. The philosopher Friedrich Nietzsche, a painfully inhibited figure in day-to-day life, declared, 'I would believe only in a God who could dance' – a comment that stands beside his equally apodictic pronouncement: 'Without music, life would be a mistake.'

Despite this recommendation from the most unlikely of sources, dancing is an activity that many of us – arguably those of us who might most need to do it – are powerfully inclined to resist and deep down to fear. We stand on the side of the dance floor, appalled at the possibility of being called to join in; we make our excuses the moment the music begins; we take pains that no one will ever, ever see our hips unite with a beat.

The point here is definitely not to learn to dance like an expert; it is to remember that dancing badly is something we might actually want to do and, equally importantly, something that we already know how to do – at least to the appalling level that is the only proficiency we need to derive key benefits.

In almost all cultures and at all points of history (except our own, oddly enough), dancing has been widely understood as a form of exercise with something very important to contribute to our mental state. Dancing has had nothing to do with dancing well, being young or revealing one's stylishness. We might summarise it like this: dancing has been valued for allowing us to transcend our individuality and for inducing us to merge into a larger, more welcoming and more redemptive whole.

Shiva as the Lord of Dance,
made in Tamil Nadu, India,
c. 950–1000.
Shiva, Lord of the Dance,
celebrates harmony with the
cosmos.

William-Adolphe Bouguereau,
The Youth of Bacchus, 1884.
A break from individualism and
reason: Dionysus (also known
as Bacchus to the Romans)
leading a dance.

One of the main gods of Hinduism was the dancing god Shiva. The meaning of Shiva's dance has a resonance far beyond a specific religion: by dancing, one may return to harmony with the cosmos. As limbs swing and bodies sway, the many details of our material and practical lives – our age, income, voting preferences, even our gender – drop away and we reunite with the totality.

A comparably rich vision of dancing developed in classical Greece. The Greeks were for the most part committed worshippers of the rational mind. Their foremost god, Apollo, was the embodiment of cool reason and disciplined wisdom. However, the Greeks understood that a life devoted only to serenity of mind could be at grave risk of desiccation and loneliness. They therefore balanced their concern with Apollo with regular festivals in honour of a quite different deity, Dionysus, a god who drank wine, stayed up late, loved music – and danced.

The Greeks knew that the more rational we usually are, the more important it is occasionally to fling ourselves around to the wild rhythms of pipes and drums. At the festivals of Dionysus, held in Athens in March every year, even the most venerable and dignified members of the community would join in the unrestrained dancing that, lubricated by generous amounts of red wine, lasted until dawn.

A word often used to describe such dancing is the telling term 'ecstatic'. This comes from the Ancient Greek word *ekstasis*: *ek* (meaning 'out') and *stasis* (meaning 'standing'), indicating a state in which we symbolically stand outside ourselves, separated from the dense, detailed and self-centred layers of our identities that we normally focus on and obsess over, and reconnect with something more primal and more necessary: our common human nature. Through a period of ecstatic dancing, we remember what it is like to belong, to be part of something larger than ourselves, to be indifferent to our own egos and to be reunited with humanity.

This aspiration hasn't entirely disappeared in modernity, but it has been assigned to very particular settings: the disco and the rave. These places often point us in unhelpful directions: towards being cool, of a certain age and knowledgeable about very modish clothes and sounds – criteria that leave many of us out. We urgently need to recover a sense of the universal benefit of dancing. The greatest enemy of this is fear; in particular, the fear that we could look like an idiot in front of people whose opinion might matter. The way through this is not to be told that we will be fine and, with a bit of effort, far from idiotic. In fact, we should accept with good grace that the whole point of redemptive, consoling and cathartic communal dancing is the chance to look like total, thoroughgoing idiots, the bigger the better, in the company of hundreds of other equally and generously publicly idiotic fellow humans.

We spend a good deal of time fearing that we might be idiots and holding back from a host of important aspirations and ambitions as a result. We could shake ourselves from such inhibitions by relinquishing any remaining sense of dignity and by accepting that we are idiotic by nature. We are great sacks of foolishness that cry in the night, bump into doors, fart in the bath and kiss people's noses by mistake. Far from being shameful and isolating, this idiocy is a basic feature of our nature that unites us with everyone else on the planet. We are idiots now, we were idiots in the past and we will be idiots in the future. There is no other option for a human.

Dancing provides us with an occasion when this basic idiocy can be publicly displayed and communally celebrated. On a dance floor filled with comparable idiots, we can at last delight in our joint foolishness; we can throw off our customary shyness and reserve and fully embrace our dazzling strangeness and derangement. An hour of frantic jigging should decisively shake us from any enduring belief in our normalcy or seriousness. We will no longer be able to bully others, persuade them of our superiority, humiliate them for their mistakes or pontificate on weighty matters. We will no longer worry how others see us or regret a few things we said to intimidating strangers. The gentle aches in our limbs and our memories of our moves will remind us of anchoring facts that will guarantee our ongoing sanity and kindness.

Whenever we have the chance to invite others around, especially very serious people by whom we are intimidated or who we might be seeking to impress, we should remember the divine Dionysus and dare, with his wisdom in mind, to put on 'Dancing Queen', 'I'm So Excited' or 'We are Family'. Knowing that we have Nietzsche on our side, we should let rip with a playlist that includes 'What a Feeling', 'Dance with Somebody' and 'It's Raining Men'. We should lose command of our normal, rational pilot selves, abandon our arms to the harmonies, throw away our belief in a 'right' way to dance or indeed to live, build the intensity of our movements to a frenzy, gyrate our heads to empty them of their absurd worries, forget our jobs, qualifications, status, achievements, plans, hopes and fears, and merge with the universe – or at

Looking like an idiot shouldn't be a risk: it's the point.

least its more immediate representatives, our fellow new, mad friends, before whom the disclosure of idiocy will be total.

Around us might be a shy accountant, an efficient dental nurse or a white-haired school principal bending up and down and flinging their arms in the air, throwing their heads back and contorting their bodies. After a few songs, something astonishing will begin to happen: it won't matter any more that we said a slightly out-of-place thing in a meeting two weeks ago, that we haven't yet met the love of our lives or that we still don't understand very much. We will feel a part of something far more important than ourselves: a supportive community in which our individual errors and doubts will cease to weigh so heavily and punishingly upon us.

Through a dance, we glimpse a huge project: how we might more regularly experience ourselves as vulnerable in front of other people in order to become better friends to ourselves and more generous and compassionate companions to others. The true potential of dancing has for too long been abandoned by thoughtful people to stylish elites who have forgotten the elemental seriousness of allowing themselves to be and look idiotic. Let's reclaim the ecstatic dance and uninhibited boogie-woogie for their deepest universal purposes: to reconnect, reassure and reunite us.

(ii) The hand of the other

We know, in theory, about valuing other people: respecting them as unique individuals, listening to their voices and accepting humanity in all its majestic diversity. The lesson has been made for us in politics. Since the inception of Athenian democracy, or at least since the French and American revolutions, we have heard much about the near-sacred rights of every citizen, about our equal standing before authority and about our universal claims to be heard and honoured. Christianity has made a comparable point in the spiritual sphere: everyone has a precious soul; everyone deserves love; we are all as unique and as precious as small children.

Yet whatever the theory, this is not quite how we live in practice. We largely dwell in suspicion of one another. We are quick to fill with anger and mistrust. We are ready to imagine the darkest things about strangers. Rarely do we surrender to benevolence or smiling tenderness towards our fellow humans.

But there might be a way to access such a mood via a physical exercise as peculiar-sounding as it may be consoling: with their consent, to take a minute to really study someone else's hand, holding it in ours and observing it with deep curiosity and imagination.

Palm readers have long known something that most of us overlook: that hands are very telling. Unfortunately, they have taken this insight into a fantastical direction, suggesting that hands can tell us the one thing that no one is ever able to know: what will happen in the future. But outside of this, their focus has surely been correct. Perhaps far more than other parts of the body, hands are supremely eloquent. We might say that if 'the soul', that confluence of deep identity, vulnerability and singularity, dwells anywhere, it is in the hands. To look closely over someone's hands, to open the palm, observe the fingers, follow the veins and examine the creases and folds, is to gain a powerful sense of the newness and exoticism of their life. It is hard not to feel sympathy and even love, in the most innocent but sincere sense.

The path from a neglect of hands to their more appropriate appreciation can be tracked in the history of art. For most of the medieval period, artists knew that humans have hands – otherwise we would have trouble holding anything up (for example, our child) – but they chose to see these organs in the most schematic and indistinct of ways. For the artist sculpting the mother of God out of walnut wood in Auvergne sometime around 1200, hands were just hands in general, not *someone's* hands in particular.

Virgin and Child in Majesty,
from Auvergne, France,
c. 1175–1200.

Giotto, detail of *Resurrection*
(*Noli me tangere*), c. 1305.

Even the Italian painter Giotto (c. 1267–1337), a genius at rendering emotion, evidently wasn't very interested in the details when depicting his characters' hands on the walls of the Scrovegni Chapel in Padua around 1300: four sausage fingers and a thumb sufficed.

In Europe, it was only when we entered the late Renaissance that artists begin to become appropriately interested in some of the things that hands have to tell us.

In one of the central works of the history of art, hands at last have a central place. The momentous moment of near contact between the human and the divine in Michelangelo's *The Creation of Adam* on the Sistine Chapel ceiling is articulated not via the mind or the eyes, but the fingers. It's not words or a smile or an embrace; all the intensity of the connection between man and god is focused on the precise position and character of two hands: on

(Top) Michelangelo, *The Creation of Adam*, c. 1508–1512. (Bottom) Detail. Here, hands become eloquent as the divine spark reaches out to animate the newly created human.

the left (human) side, more drawn in and languid; on the right (godly) side, more open, assertive and commanding. Fortuitously, in the decades after Michelangelo finished his labours, the plaster between the hands of the two central figures began to crack, creating a sense of ever-widening and poignant division in the relationship between the heavenly and the human.

Edgar Degas, *Study of Hands*,
c. 1860. This eloquent study is
sublimely expressive of the whole
character of the sitter.

The idea of studying hands closely perhaps reached its highest point of development in the 19th century. A great artist such as Edgar Degas (1834–1917) might paint a pair of otherwise disembodied hands and leave us to fill in the entirety of the complex individual they belonged to, confident that, from these hints, we would have enough to imagine a whole life story.

Study any hand carefully enough, the artists appeared to be telling us, and you can learn the crucial elements of what matters in an individual.

We might try a similar exercise with an old or, more daringly, a new friend. Once this hand was tiny; it struggled to grasp a raisin. Probably they sucked their thumb; their fingers would have pulled up zips and undone buttons on their mother's cardigan. Their hand has been employed in their most intimate activities. It's been clenched in anger; it's wiped away tears; the fingernails have dug into the palm at moments of anxiety; it's signed documents; made graphically rude gestures; it's clutched a wall in terror; it's been held by a parent before crossing a road. One day an undertaker will fold it carefully across this person's chest.

Through the study of a hand, we feel at an emotional level what might otherwise have remained an intellectual notion: that another person is just as complex, strange and multifaceted as we are; that they, like us, are the centres of their own bewilderingly rich and precious perceptions, and are every bit as worthy of consideration and sympathy. Once we look back up at their eyes after time with their hand, they might never be the same person again – in the best of ways.

We speak so much of universal brother- and sisterhood. But it isn't until we have spent some moments immersed in the stories whispered by another's hands that we stand to be able to turn an abstract aspiration into something properly useful and humanising.

(iii) Sofa jumping

Adult social life labours under an arduous rule: that the better we want to get to know someone, the more serious the topics we raise with them should be. It might be acceptable to discuss the weather with a passing acquaintance, but when it comes to opening ourselves up to someone else and discovering their profound selves in turn, then we should head for the graver themes of existence: what we want to get out of our careers; what motivates us in relationships; how we assess our families; what politics should aim for. In this view, seriousness of mind is the royal road to friendship.

However, if self-disclosure and familiarity are really the underlying goals, we may have to study more closely the behaviour and wisdom of small children – in particular their insight that one cannot claim to know anyone well until the body has been closely engaged in the process of acquaintanceship.

Young children are often daringly uninterested in conversation. When breaking the ice with a new companion, they will skirt politics, they won't discuss the stock market, they will avoid consideration of family history or upcoming holidays. With the lack of respect for precedent that comes more naturally to someone newly arrived on the planet, they will try to do something physical even before names have been exchanged. When they are especially inspired, they might head for one of the most legendary bodily exercises of all: sofa jumping.

They will clamber up onto the nearest sofa, perhaps raising it in height by adding a few cushions, and then take a flying leap onto the floor, seeing how far they can land – and in particular, how much further than their new teammate. If the situation is auspicious, there will be a well-polished wooden floor or glossy tiles that will allow for skidding and the clearing of some remarkable distances.

The notion of being an adult is understandably linked to the idea of being serious. There is so much that we have to be responsible for, so many troubling facts that claim our attention and so many potential difficulties to which we must be permanently alert.

Seriousness becomes a hidden enemy in getting on with other people properly, because our rational, thoughtful and controlled selves are only a limited part of who we really are. Yet meeting a person with due gravity is doomed to give us a distorted impression of them – and, equally, to convey a very unrepresentative slice of us.

A commitment to seriousness limits us too in terms of who we feel we might get on with. We become restricted to the subsection of the world that shares our intellectual concerns, aesthetic orientations and psychological dispositions – as well as our preferred ways of discussing these. We prioritise the most erudite contents of our minds as the basis for our social existence. Practically no one else thinks about intellectual issues precisely as we do, yet many people remain highly viable friends. In other words, we will be committing ourselves to loneliness.

Instead of letting our mental prowess guide our friendships, we should let the body be the ambassador of intimacy. By current standards, it is ridiculous for a group of adults to clamber, one by one, onto a sofa in their socks and to strive with every muscle to take the largest leap of which they are capable, or to swing their arms backwards and make themselves into a rocket or a plane and attempt to land with some of the bounce and grace of a kangaroo or gazelle, while collapsing far nearer to their launch pad than they would have wished into an indecorous, giggling and slightly bruised heap.

Nor is there anything especially respectable about growing competitive in the course of such a game, about getting into technical disputes with other participants (Were the jumper's legs properly together as they leapt? Were they together when they landed?) and scouring the kitchen for some tape to mark everyone's landing spots. But at the same time, seldom could silliness be more important.

We often do things that, later, we judge to have been absurd and ridiculous. We wince at how we could have been such numbskulls and vow never to embarrass ourselves again. But the true way out of embarrassment is not to attempt to expunge it from our routines; it is to orchestrate occasions when it can have an honoured place in our social lives.

Calculated, on-purpose silliness means willingly abandoning our minds' overly rigid notions of dignity. We should strive to be adult enough to consent – for a while – to the claims of childhood, a period of our lives when we knew blessedly little about house prices and what Picasso thought of capitalism.

Sofa jumping has a power to transform our relationships with others because, at last, we've been idiots *together.* Instead of our foolishness (which we try

Fig. 1
Sofa jumping

so hard to keep secret) being a barrier to connection and the grounds for shame and blushing, it becomes an arena in which we can meet as equals. Fortunately, we can't ever take someone entirely seriously again after we have seen them screwing up their eyes before taking a leap or eagerly disputing just how far they've jumped across the room as compared to their opponents. In other words, after sofa jumping, we can't ever treat them with unimaginative indifference again.

Part of the enormous appeal of sex is its power to change the dynamics of a relationship with another person. After we have seen someone naked, perhaps on all fours, writhing in pleasure, after we have caressed the intimate zones of their body and seen them passionately interested in a few parts of ours, we know them in a wholly new way. There will be a complicity between us: smiles will come more readily, as will forgiveness and tenderness. It won't matter so much that they might earn far more than we do or have studied a great deal longer; we will in important ways be allies and soulmates.

For practical (though sometimes slightly sad) reasons, we aren't able to have sex with very many people in the course of our lives. And yet the quest for greater intimacy and connection that to a significant extent powers our sexual appetites is capable of being deployed elsewhere. It would be tragic if all our longings for warmth would forever have to pass through the narrow gate of sex. Fortunately, through the game of sofa jumping, we have another, far more available, chance to build up the connections we long for. No true encounter should be complete without at least a few rounds.

(iv) Dinner table orchestra

One of the most astonishing and moving of all sights is that of a well-practised orchestra working together to perform a great symphonic masterpiece. Along with forty-seven other equally focused colleagues, Sigrid will be sawing away at the violin, Jai-wu bellowing into a trombone and Kaspar pounding the timpani – but the result will be the opposite of chaos. Despite every human remaining an unfathomable, self-focused individual, for a time the members of an orchestra are able to generate a sublime sense of harmony. Their collective work stands as a beguiling metaphor for what we would ideally want social life to be like: a setting in which every person can make their own unique contribution in a beautifully coordinated way to a noble, overarching whole.

This kind of coherence is one we normally despair of experiencing ourselves, unless we started on the viola at seven and are deft at following a conductor's baton. At the same time, we know that when friends are gathered around the dinner table, each person's individuality too often leads to disagreement and discord, or at least incomprehension and boredom. We may love our friends, but it is rarely easy to access a feeling of collective harmony.

There is an exercise that can allow us to experience the kind of cohesion that the members of an orchestra will generate but that does not require us to practise for four hours a day for twelve years. One person starts by knocking out a steady beat on the table with their hand. The person next to them then strikes a fork (very gently) on a wine glass to a different rhythm. The person beside them uses their plate as a delicate drum, carefully banging their knife against the rim in a complementary beat. The next individual has the job of letting out a 'hmmm' sound in time with the knife, and another person joins in with an occasional 'nananah … nananah'. Gradually, a little social miracle occurs: by an ingrained social instinct, we collectively cohere around a harmonious tone. We've started an orchestra; we're making music; we are almost 'one'.

It is a useful strategy to try something along these lines quite early on in the evening, just for a quarter of an hour or so, especially if a few of the guests are potentially agitated or querulous. The experience of being part of an ensemble has a lingering effect. It's not so easy to get irritated by someone's view on public holidays or the American Civil War if, only a little while before, you've been happily nanah-ing and plate clinking together.

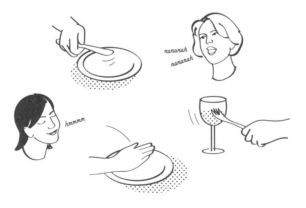

Fig. 2
Dinner table orchestra

(v) **The blind car**

The foremost cement of friendship is *trust*, defined as an impression that if one day we had to be vulnerable in front of someone (weak, scared, in pain or in need), we could rely on them; they would prove kind, loyal, non-judgemental, generous and sensitive enough not to cause us humiliation. We could outline a peculiarity in our personal life and they would listen with sympathy, offer intelligent, unpatronising counsel and not tell a soul. We could be in a temporary financial jam and they would recognise our underlying decency and tide us over until we recovered. We might need to have an operation and they would offer to come around and change our bandages.

The problem with trust is not that there aren't people who deserve it, but that there are not so many occasions on which it can be nurtured. There aren't many moments when we are flung back on the kindness of friends and strangers. For a long time, we don't have embarrassing secrets, money problems or bodily aches, and aren't called upon to lean on others for assistance. However, in order to fertilise our friendships, we should engineer situations where, for a while, within the context of an exercise, we learn to give someone else the keys to our integrity and safety and find out what it can be like to be in a risky spot and treated with kindness and consideration.

A useful exercise for this is called the blind car. In a largeish room with a number of people in it, everyone should team up with a partner. One of us is the driver, the other the passenger. The passenger is asked to keep their eyes closed throughout the game, and the driver stands behind them and places their hands on either side of their waist. The driver 'steers' the passenger by squeezing them once on both sides in order to go, twice in order to stop and once on either side to steer left or right. Many other 'cars' are set in motion at the same time. The idea is for a group of cars to circulate around the room as far and as fast as possible but without colliding, despite the evident risks that they might do so and the jeopardy that a collision might be rather painful.

A lot of the blind passengers will be going 'ahhh' and letting out small 'yikes' as the game progresses.

The level of trust required to play is not huge. At worst, one ends up with a bruise, but it is still unusual – and salutary – to place oneself at the mercy of a 'driver' with whom one is for a time helpless and blind. The game itself might only last a short while – fifteen minutes or so – but its value will lie in what happens afterwards. We will have had an experience in which none of our normal defences and capabilities will have been available, and where we are forced to rely on the foresight and solicitude of someone else. We will have experienced the kind of trust we will one day sorely need, long before we really need it.

Fig. 3
The blind car

[vi] Horizontal conversation

At the dawn of psychoanalysis, Sigmund Freud made a remarkable discovery: that there can be an immense difference between what someone will tell you when they are sitting opposite you in a chair, looking at you in the eye, and what they will tell you when they are lying flat on their back, looking up at the ceiling.

Freud's goal was for his patients to be honest with him, to divulge their true selves with as little inhibition as possible, for it was their self-ignorance and denial that, in his view, were the ultimate causes of their illnesses. A capacity to be honest was not merely refreshing; it might make the difference between sanity and despair.

The benefits of staring at the ceiling: Sigmund Freud's couch, transported from Vienna to London in the year before his death in 1939.

Freud also came to realise how much his own presence could be responsible for inhibiting his clients from reporting candidly on their dreams and fantasies. Something about seeing his face and feeling his eyes on them meant that patients were inclined to disguise their true selves. They would hold back from the more embarrassing or sensitive material of their lives and attempt to appear more 'normal' than was true or good for them. Freud recognised just how much opposition there could be to talking in an unvarnished way about incest, cross-dressing, castration, impotence, cannibalism, anal sex or murder while sitting face to face, as one might in a Viennese café or a standard doctor's surgery. Hence his decision, taken in 1890, to shift his patients onto a couch, which has become a mainstay of psychotherapeutic consulting rooms the world over.

Perhaps more than we realise, seeing another person's face can discourage us from a confession: we edit our self-presentation in the light of their reactions; we hold back from accessing the properly interesting, complicated and troubling (and therefore important) parts of ourselves. This happens in consulting rooms, but it happens just as often in the far more familiar context of the dinner party or social gathering. Here too, though we have come together ostensibly to be sincere and speak honestly about our lives, we may succumb to a fear of sharing what is truly going on inside us. Feeling eyes on us, we hold back from divulging our reality. We flinch at putting others off; we follow every twitch of their mouths and censor ourselves in line with what we imagine (often quite unfairly) to be their appetite for judgement and distaste. As a result, we may spend far longer than any of us want circling what happened on a recent holiday or how the house renovations are going, when there might be so much else we would like to share.

With Freud's example in mind, we should pioneer our own forms of horizontal conversation. After dessert or between courses, we might suggest that we all go and lie down somewhere on the floor. It might be on blankets or on the carpet; it could happen in the kitchen or the hall. We might find it useful to switch off the lights.

It can be a strange sensation, to be stretched out in a darkened space with people – some of whom we may not know well – with an open invitation to free-associate about our lives. We might all stay silent for two minutes to adjust to the situation. In those moments, we might think about the broad structure of our years: once we were babies, then toddlers. We went to school and it felt as if it would go on forever. Then we started work, travelled, had relationships, made some big mistakes, were thrilled and sometimes despaired – and now it's now. We'll get older, and eventually – not as far away as we would like – we will die. We become newly conscious of voices, our own and those of others; we can hear so many more of the nuances when we aren't also being called to look, or constantly to ensure our own expression hasn't developed in gormless or bored directions.

In the dark, it matters less what other people might think of us. We can be more loyal to ourselves. In the process, while examining the light fittings in the gloom, we can do other people the ultimate social favour: letting them see our vulnerability and peculiarity, which can appease their own sense of oddity and loneliness.

Fig. 4
Horizontal conversation

We might broach some of the following sensitive themes:

- What I'm scared of is ...

- A thing that was tricky in my childhood was ...

- At work I have difficulties around ...

- I feel lonely when ...

- I'm so ashamed that ...

- What I'd love more than anything is ...

- If only I wasn't so scared, I would ...

- If it didn't seem so selfish, I would ...

- If I couldn't fail, I would ...

By lying down in a strange way after dinner, we're not drifting towards eccentricity. We're using an unusual manoeuvre to do something very sensible that we have aspired to do for a long time: to tell other people what it is like to be us, and to hear individually strange but collectively deeply liberating truths from others about how they're getting on with the always puzzling business of being alive.

(vii) The cleaning party

We often imagine that we can receive our friends only when we have cleared away most of what we normally are: when we've hidden the sweets and the half-eaten crisps, when we've tidied up the magazines and jumpers, when we've slipped our tear-stained diary under the bed, fluffed up the cushions and put together an unrepresentative meal consisting of three courses, dark chocolate truffles, an Italian wine and a mint tea infusion. This, we believe, is what will best enable us to be known, accepted and liked.

The impulse is understandable but also poignantly counterproductive. We spend so much of our time striving to be 'normal' and – as we believe – more like the people we admire, but we fail to notice how much we are disguising our reality and constructing a front that is more likely to intimidate than reassure others. If the impulse behind friendship is a longing to be seen and for the true nature of our lives to be understood with generosity, then it is paradoxical that so many of the social encounters we choreograph are staged and guaranteed not to foster the self-revealing intimacy we seek.

Rather than creating an artful 'false self' for public occasions, we would be wiser and more daring to use gatherings specifically to show the people we are drawn to what our lives are truly like. Instead of the standard dinner party, we might invite our friends to a cleaning party: an evening where we present our dwelling exactly as it normally is, and – for good measure – ask our friends if they might accompany us in a spot of light but thorough housekeeping.

Together we might empty out the fridge, change the beds, vacuum the living room and sort out books into 'keepers' and 'charity shop' piles, before sitting on stools and cracking open some tins of baked beans. Rather than insisting on a shiny normalcy and intimidating others with our seamless existence, we might openly display the mess in our clothes cupboards and ask our friends for help in hanging up our trousers.

However pleasant it may be to do nothing very much with someone other than sit on the sofa and sip some wine, it can be far more beneficial to a union to set to work on a task; to have a job to do. This is why it is generally much easier to get close to people at university than in later life. University friends will end up doing so much more with us: together we'll make beds, go to the laundromat, struggle to cook a chicken – and, in the process, we'll laugh, penetrate each other's social defences and see each other as fellow vulnerable, suffering humans. There is a limit to how well we can get to know someone whom we will only ever sit with in a coffee shop.

Without anything deceitful being meant, much of the reality of our lives is under-represented in the picture of ourselves we give to others. We appear far more competent, focused, respectable, domestic and unpanicked than we are. We think it is polite to plaster over our imperfections – and, to an extent, it may be. But, in the long term, it means that we are continuously implying that we may be someone other than we are to those we care most about.

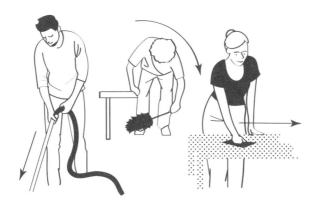

Fig. 5
Light housekeeping with friends

In reality, everyone spends time pairing socks, crying, shopping for groceries, vacuuming, eating junk food, thinking of their death and taking out the bins. We might imagine it to be insulting to invite a good friend around and then hand them a toilet brush. But it is a gesture of the truest kind of friendship: a chance for another person to step into the reality of our lives and to know us for who we really are.

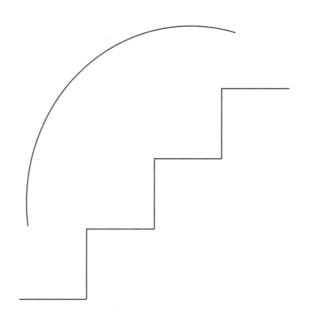

CONFIDENCE

Introduction

To a dramatic extent, our success in life does not depend on talent alone. A sizeable, even decisive, contribution is made by that highly elusive and emotional factor: our degree of confidence in ourselves.

Self-confidence is not the conviction that we're bound to succeed at everything we try. The belief that we can't fail is an irrational delusion bound eventually to lead to disaster. Genuine confidence is precisely the opposite: the inner sureness that we'll be OK even if we fail quite a few times or don't pull off what we're aiming at. To the confident person, the stakes are manageable, which leaves them free to try the many interesting things in the world where success cannot be guaranteed.

At the core of a properly confident mentality is a sense that trying and making mistakes are integral parts of the process of mastery. The people who look highly competent now must have stumbled many times. Failure is no sign that we must lose in the end.

True confidence builds on an idea that embarrassing ourselves is normal at the start of anything worthwhile. We should see that messing up is a standard feature of the human condition, not a strange failing of our own. It should never keep us from the chance to become more competent in the future, since every person whose competence we admire once began from a position of weakness. We learn to get good at things not by never finding them difficult, but by developing the right sort of attitude towards difficulty.

The challenge is to give ourselves physical experiences that can turn these theoretical ideas into reality. Fortunately, there are plenty of exercises that can help.

Singing

Most of what we would really like to do is annihilated long before birth by a masochistic sense of our own incompetence. We can't possibly invite people to dinner at home *because we're not really great cooks*; we can't show anyone the poem we've written *because it's not quite right yet*; we won't strip off and dive into the sea *because our body is not in beach shape*. We would so much like to love, live, be free, be authentic, but ...

Few activities fit more neatly into this category of throttled aspiration than singing. How much we would like to give it a go, but how well we anticipate our likely absurdity. We're reluctant even to try to string a few notes together in solitude. We could be walking in a desert and still feel anxious about humming, so deeply have we internalised a worry about judgement.

This is a particular pity because singing is one of the most basic forms of expression at which no one could ever – in any *a priori* way – be bad. Our remote ancestors probably sang before they could speak; as babies we responded to lullabies long before we could comprehend words.

Many societies have made collective singing a central part of communal existence. Nowadays, even the remaining fragments of opportunity – in a church or on the football terraces – are often inaccessible; some part of us might long to join in and merge our own weak and out-of-tune voice with the crowd, but these occasions can feel as if they belong to others whose outlook and convictions we don't directly share.

The ideal collective anthem has an easy enough, forgiving tune, enabling us to follow the phrasing and the lilt of the melody, even if (to an expert ear) we're never quite in key. It also expresses ideas that are meaningful to us.

Some good options for a singing exercise include:

Encouragement: The Beatles' 'Hey Jude'
Kindness: Mozart's aria 'Blow gently, you breezes' from Act I of *Cosi fan tutte*
Universality: Beethoven's 'Ode to Joy'

In a singing ritual, the words should be printed out and distributed, and someone should take us quickly through the tune so we've all got the basics. The lights should be lowered to create a sense of occasion; an awesome amplifier should be on hand to power things on, and then the music should be let loose. After a familiar introductory melody, we'd be given the signal to start. Of course we would lose the timing of the words, we would put the stresses on the wrong points at times, our breathing would be all askew – but we'd be doing it. We'd be soaring.

Admiration isn't enough: we need to participate with our own authentic and far-from-perfect voices.

We'd be aware, as we were singing, that others were believing the same things; they, like us, would be breaking through the barriers of embarrassment and awkwardness to join with us in creating a superlative collective moment.

From this point of view, the greatest glory of collective singing isn't a performance by a famous choir. It is in the back room of a pub or around a campfire or in someone's house, when people who can't really sing manage to sing together, and *what* they sing gives collective voice to the buried longings in their lonely, yearning hearts.

We're encountering a fundamental idea: that we don't need to be good at something for us to join in; we belong here anyway, we deserve to exist. Others are like us much more than we think: they're not judging us harshly most of the time; they're wishing that they could take the step we're taking. They are finding some of the encouragement they need in our own inept, gloriously out-of-key but genuine choral efforts.

(ii) The regression ball

We sometimes cause ourselves a lot of pain by pretending to be competent, all-knowing, proficient adults, long after we should have raised the white flag. We suffer a bitter rejection in love, but tell ourselves and the world that we'll be fine, and continue as if nothing much had happened. We hear some wounding rumours about us, but refuse to stoop to our opponents' level and plough on. We find we can't sleep at night and are exhausted and anxious in the day, but stepping aside for a break is not really our style.

It's at times like these that we should remember an exercise of the body with a power to assuage our unhelpful rigidity and restore our mental wellbeing: in response to a sense of dread or crisis, we should, without any embarrassment or compunction, curl ourselves up into a very small ball, as tightly as possible, and, if necessary, pull a blanket or duvet over our head and body. We should remain this way, fairly still and very warm, for an hour or more.

Fig. 6
The regression ball

We all originally came from a very tight, ball-like space. For the first nine months of our existence, we were curled up, with our head on our knees, protected from a more dangerous and cold world beyond by the position of our limbs. In our young years, we knew well enough how to recover this ball position when things got tough. If we were mocked in the playground or misunderstood by a snappy parent, it was instinctive to go up to our room and adopt the ball position until matters started to feel more manageable again.

Only later, around adolescence, did some of us lose sight of this valuable exercise in regression and thereby began missing out on a chance for nurture and recovery.

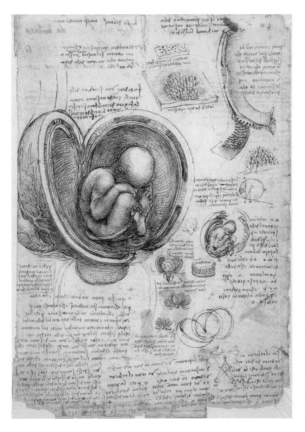

Leonardo da Vinci, *Studies of the Foetus in the Womb*, c. 1511. We have all come from a ball position, but only some of us remember to return there on a regular basis.

It is to our detriment that we have such entrenched habits of judging ourselves by the exacting standard of non-existent beings. Our notions of what can be expected of a wise, fully mature adult lack any sense of realism or kindness. Without any grounding in the truths of human nature, we insist that we should always be patient, strong, competent and in control. We forget that though we may be 28 or 47 on the outside, we are still carrying around a child version of ourselves within, for whom a day at the office will be exhausting, who won't be able to calm down easily after an insult, who will need reassurance after even a minor rejection, who will want to cry without even knowing why and who will regularly require a chance to be held like the baby we once were.

True adulthood knows how much the child within oneself still needs. There is nothing humiliating about owning up to the demands of the fragile 2-year-old we are never far from being. We need to lend our pervasive and ongoing immaturity a safe and regular berth. Doing so should be the starting point for generosity towards the more childlike sides of others as well, for they too – whatever their age or position (boss, partner, enviable rival) – will be struggling with emotions that flout adult expectations – an idea that should lessen their power to intimidate or depress us.

A functioning society would, alongside more obviously reasonable practices like yoga and jogging, allow room for its members to curl up very still into tight balls for a long time, until the adult world feels more or less bearable once again.

(iii) The pillow fight

One of the reasons why we may lack confidence is that we suffer from an awkward relationship with our own assertiveness. Being confident involves standing up for oneself and feeling that it's OK to cause another person momentary inconvenience for a worthwhile reason.

There are many things that can get in the way of arriving at a comfortable level of assertive confidence. Perhaps at an important phase in our development we felt aggressive and became horrified by our potential for destructiveness. In response, we shut down all signs of assertion. We felt it would be safer and better to be trampled on by others than to hold our corner, which became confused with lashing out. Or maybe we had to spend significant time around someone who came across as fragile: the least insistence on our part, however reasonable, could have been enough to cause them great distress or to infuriate them. As a consequence, we learnt to muffle our needs, to keep quiet about our ideas, to demur, to accommodate and to step aside. At the time, we were only trying to survive, but we internalised a vision of existence in which there was no legitimate opportunity to press forward our own concerns. This timidity – learnt under dire pressure – may continue to dominate our lives even when circumstances change significantly. We still act as if everyone around us might react like one or two difficult or troubled individuals we encountered long ago.

For all this, we might try a little pillow-fighting exercise. Two or more players should equip themselves with big, soft pillows and aim to thwack each other as energetically as possible for seven minutes on the shoulders, back, buttocks and legs.

Hitting hard is important. Your blows should make solid, satisfying contact, for you know that you can't conceivably hurt anyone with a pillow. You're being boisterous rather than aggressive and your fellow players are prepared. They don't resent you for trying to whack them with a pile of feathers; they're trying to do that to you too. We're getting a visceral, physical experience that translates into a key psychological idea: you can assert yourself without being a bully; you can express yourself forcefully without in any way wanting to humiliate the other person; you can robustly stand your ground, or press insistently forwards, and be appreciated by those you engage with, without prompting tears.

Via our flailing pillows, we're physically rehearsing a central need of the mature mind that applies universally in our dealings with others: fighting our corner isn't dangerous and, when delivered with good humour and good will, a solid blow to the other will create a friend rather than an enemy.

Fig. 7
Pillow fight

(iv) Hip swinging

The hip is one of the places where crippling self-consciousness may easily get entrenched, for to thrust out one's hip, flex a buttock or raise an arm over the head can seem like a declaration of sexiness that can feel deeply awkward and vulgar to us.

And yet, feeling that one's sexual nature is valid and potentially intriguing – not something to be permanently kept in the shadows – is at the core of self-acceptance and of a wider sense of legitimacy, where the potential responses of others aren't terrifying and anxiety doesn't get to close down the more seductive displays of who we are.

It can feel as if hip movements belong only to people whom we might admire from a distance, but with whom we feel limited intimate, intellectual or spiritual kinship. Sexiness, and the confidence that goes with it, may – in our imagination – always be the preserve of others, some of whom are on stage in Las Vegas.

But there's another, much less overt history of the hip. In classical Greek culture, hip swinging was associated with Apollo, god of art and reason.

In the most sacred precinct of the ancient Western world, on the island of Delos, stood a statue of Apollo with his right hip thrust out and his right arm (we can suppose, because the limb has been lost for centuries) arching above his head. It's an image of being sexy and wise at the same time, physically provocative as well as interested in rational investigation, happy to be seen as filled with desire and longing and yet also dignified and alive to all the countervailing values of existence.

In honour of Apollo, you should stand with your feet a few inches apart and your toes slightly turned out (at 10 o'clock and 2 o'clock). Slowly and gently

(Right) Marble statue of Apollo,
from Cyrene, Libya, c. 2nd century
BCE. Apollo: My hips mean grace
of mind, noble simplicity and calm
grandeur.

(Left) A kind of hip swinging that only
the very brave would dare.

bend your right knee. Your heel will rise up and you'll feel your toes coming into contact with the floor; then thrust your left hip out to the side. Exaggerate the movement and see how far you can push the hip out. There's a tendency for one shoulder to lift as you do this, but try to keep both shoulders level. It's useful to do this exercise standing in front of a mirror.

Now transfer your weight to the other side. Bend the other leg in the same way as before and the other hip will loosen and stick out. After you've done this for a few days and the movement starts to feel natural, extend the exercise by twisting the extended hip forwards.

The deliberate, exaggerated movement of the pelvis indicates that we're not intimidated by our fears of what others might think of us. We can allow ourselves to be deliberately alluring and provocative, even if we are only enacting the move in the privacy of our bathroom.

At a daring moment, give the movement a small, quiet try in public – maybe standing in line at the shops or at the airport carousel. You'll be learning that you can try being charming, enticing and provocative, and no one will mind. You will be on the way to discovering a confidence that was always your due.

(v) The dressing-up game

Almost all children derive huge satisfaction from dressing up and spending a few hours as a Viking warrior, a firefighter or a Native American princess. But as we get older, most of us grow uncomfortable around the idea of wearing clothes that don't match the identity we feel an allegiance to. If we open the doors of a typical grown-up wardrobe, we're not likely to find the garb of an 18th-century French *philosophe*, a Roman toga, Elizabeth the First's ceremonial gown or a firefighter's uniform – alongside the normal work and casual wear.

We tell ourselves that it doesn't make much sense to dress up as someone we're obviously not. It would be undignified and ridiculous for a modern-day accountant or lawyer to don the armour of a medieval knight or the tunic of a prerevolutionary Russian peasant.

However, our seemingly reasonable attitude may reflect a mistaken and flattened conception of identity. It's understandable that we think of character as a relatively simple, enduring and stable phenomenon, defined by our jobs, our gender, where we live, the era we were born into and our relationship status. We have one name and should logically be more or less one thing. The truth, however, tends to be more complicated and interesting. Whatever the unitary identity we strive to project to the world, a vast number of 'characters' jostle for attention and expression inside each of us. There are parts of us that are younger and others that are older than the date on our passports; there are richer and poorer figures too, and some that date from centuries very distant from our own. There may be bits of an Egyptian pharaoh in us, or of a medieval Irish monk or an early 20th-century French ballet dancer. Buried within our minds, we contain alternative people we could have been had we lived under different circumstances or been encouraged in alternative ways: a person who might have liked to worship at an altar or who might have wanted solitude and a simpler outdoor life; someone who might have spoken German or been a courtier to the emperor of China. To know our full identities means owning up to the multiple selves we harbour within and, if possible, working out ways of giving a few of them an occasional chance for expression.

One of the best ways to do this is dressing-up exercises. Clothes provide the most immediate and intimate kinds of access to our alternative dimensions. There are costumes that temporarily but usefully emphasise aspects of our personalities that were squeezed out of ordinary life but that benefit from being acknowledged.

'The Pirate'

When I am dressed as a pirate I can reject responsibility, be on the wrong side of the law, feel the thrill of cursing and swearing and relish the idea that I might have told my parents to sod off and run away from home aged 15.

This isn't anything like the whole of who I am: I lived with my mother until I was 27 and I work in local government. It's just a little bit of who I might have been; the rest of me has something to learn from occasionally exploring this version.

'The 18th century Parisian'

My work in the legal rights department is important to me, but I get a wider perspective on myself (and on the lives of others) by inhabiting the clothes and mentality of a fashionable Parisian from the 1700s.

Dressed like this, I can feel more sympathy with kinds of people I'd normally be wary of (i.e., people who have lots of advantages). I also become more confident; I feel like I want to make witty put-downs and dazzle a little. What I'd really like is to take these things back to my day-to-day existence – and I think that's starting to happen.

'The Cave-dweller'

I've always lived in the suburbs – and in general I like it – but I'm also drawn to the idea of fending for myself, having to make everything I use (I made this costume, by the way) and imagining myself without any of the comforts and conveniences I usually take for granted. It gives you a weird perspective on other people: you realise that we're all still cave-dwellers in a way, just with suits and hairdryers. Probably the same emotions are going around today that were going around then: jealousy, pride, fear, hope – the basic stuff.

'The Judge'

The funny thing is that in much of my life I've had difficulty with authority – my dad, the teachers at school, a series of bosses. But when I put on my pretend robes I can – in a small way – get in touch with an authoritarian trait in me. There's a part of me that likes the idea of being in charge; it's just I haven't been able to access it very well normally. It sounds a bit mad, but I feel I've been playing at being meek all my life and now I'm starting to feel more comfortable with the idea that maybe sometimes people could listen to me.

'The Crossdresser'

I'm Dave the rest of the time and David at conferences. It's nice to feel flirty and light, to swirl around and kick up one's heels – and maybe this kind of fun doesn't always have to mean having a female chromosome. I don't think anyone in the aerospace business would guess I do this, but I wouldn't necessarily mind them finding out. For a long while, I was desperately ashamed. Now I just treat it as one more interesting thing about being human. The way I see it, why should only one gender know about the pleasures of Chanel Rouge Noir nail varnish?

—

A man putting on women's clothes, or a suburban mother dressing up as a cave-dweller, doesn't represent who they 'really' are. The very basis of dressing-up games is the idea that we are never in essence one thing; the game just provides a brief excursion into elements of being that have been excessively segregated in the rest of life.

If we have never done such an exercise, we should first ask ourselves what we would want to try out if we had free rein. It may take a while for us to develop an idea, and we might smile from embarrassment, but our eventual answer will tell us something important about neglected sides of us.

We might then practise dressing up in relatively covert ways; it might just mean getting hold of a certain sort of shoe, bracelet, watch or hat. Others around us might not even realise the game we're playing, but we will know that we are taking important steps towards broadening who we can allow ourselves to be.

Our societies look on with admiration at someone with an intellectual interest in early human settlements, the experience of other genders, the workings of the legal system or the politics of France in the 18th century – why shouldn't the putting on of a wig or a dress, an animal hide or a necklace belong to a no less worthy and no less logically connected adventure of discovery?

(vi) Swearing in the woods

We're tempted to swear (even if only under our breath) many times in the course of our daily lives: when the car ahead of us stalls just as the lights turn; when our partner is twenty-six minutes late (already) even though they promised that this time they'd be punctual; when we're just settling down in a café to do some work and realise we've forgotten to charge the laptop; when there's a particularly wrong-headed article in the newspaper.

But in a curious way, our ire is misdirected. We're maddened by a specific detail when the real cause of our frustration is much grander and more general. It is, in essence, the human condition – the metaphysics of life – that distresses us so much and with which we are constantly colliding. We are fated never to be far from fury and sadness:

- As physical human beings, we are profoundly vulnerable; our organs are a fragile network just waiting to give out catastrophically at a time of their choosing.

- We have insufficient information upon which to make most major life decisions; we are steering more or less blind.

- We can imagine so much more than we have, and we live in mobile-driven, mediatised societies where envy and restlessness are constants.

- The efforts we put into securing our careers and our finances are as nothing to the heartless, fickle and destructive workings of the capitalist economic engine.

- We rely for our self-esteem and sense of comfort on the love of people we cannot control and whose needs and hopes will never align seamlessly with our own.

- We are burdened by the traumas and difficulties of complex personal histories that unconsciously distort all our reactions to current situations.

- We are subject to the random workings of fate, which have no connection whatever to justice or happiness.

The German philosopher Arthur Schopenhauer (1788–1860) labelled such issues the 'metaphysical torments' of being human; he likened them to 'design faults' in the original construction of the human animal, a creature seemingly expressly designed by nature to suffer and lament without end. But Schopenhauer urged us not to feel miserable about this or that irritant, not to obsess over the stupidity of one particular spouse or one specific colleague, one government or one nation. We were instead to focus outwards from our own travails and more rightly curse the whole basis of existence and the very structure of cosmic reality.

As Schopenhauer's great hero, the ancient Roman sage Seneca (c. 4 BCE–65 CE), asked: 'Why cry over parts of life? The whole of existence calls for tears.' He could, with even greater relevance, have said: 'Why swear at a specific irritant, when it's the whole of life that needs to be told to fuck off?'

Persuaded by the importance of acknowledging metaphysical misery head on, we should ritualise our insight, at an appointed time, with a few fellow suffering humans in tow. We should head off into the woods, out of earshot of more respectable company, and there perform a highly cathartic exercise. We should lift our heads to the sky, take a deep breath, fly high over the memories of every wrong that's ever been done to us, every mistake we've ever made, every romantic hope that's ever been dashed, everything that went awry in our childhood and education and every ridiculous thing we've ever said and done. We should gather all this into a mighty feeling of non-specific rage with which we should then shout as loudly as we can:

Fuck you, existence, you bastard cunt!
Fuck you, human nature,
Fuck the fucking cosmos,

Fuck the Big Fucking Bang.

Fuck you, time and your fucking sadism.

Fuck you, nature, that makes us all shits and fucking fools.

Fuck fucking that's meant to be so fucking great and fucks up our whole fucking lives.

Fuck the fact that we'll get fucking old, unless we fucking die fucking first.

Fuck self-consciousness that drives us fucking mad.

Fuck God who must be fucking deranged to have made this fucking shithole

and who doesn't fucking exist any-fucking-way.

Fuck me, fuck you, fuck everyone.

Fuck, fuck, fuck!

We're all so fucking fucked.

(N.B. This choral ode gains in poignancy if one refrains from employing impolite language in day-to-day life.)

We don't have to go to a literal forest for this session of cosmic swearing, but it is the ideal symbolic location. To the classical Ancient Roman imagination, the woods and forests represented the opposite of the city. In the city, there were law courts, shops, elegant houses, fine temples, schools, baths; but beyond the walls of the Empire, in the wild woodlands of Germany, fearsome tribes enacted mysterious and primitive ceremonies. They would congregate around special trees and howl at the stars, cut symbols into the trunks and make sacrifices to their savage gods. The Romans believed that one could only ever be on a single side of this divide: either one was a citizen of the Empire, at home in the city, or one was a barbarian, crouching in the dark clearings of the primeval forest. But for us, it may be necessary to be creatures of both worlds. We need the artificial refinements of the city, but we also need to commune with our uncivilised selves – that is, with the parts of who we are that are crushed and dismayed by the demands of ordered, careful, rational existence and need occasionally to let out an unrestrained, fearsome howl.

It's not enough to try this exercise only once. Our animal nature is governed – as in so many respects – by a cycle of rising tension and a growing need for release. After a cursing session, we can return from the woods calm and satiated; for a time, we can look with tender indulgence on the follies of our partner and coworkers; we can be gentle, relaxed and generous at the little inconveniences of bureaucracy and government. But then the sap of anger will rise once more: the moron from marketing will intervene at length; a parent will trap us in an unwelcome commitment; our partner won't concede a point. Soon enough, it will be time to return to the woods and lend our fucking pain another chance to echo through the bloody pine trees.

Introduction

The modern world offers us a range of opportunities and excitements from which it would be nonsensical to want to retreat. However, in some areas we have bought our advantages at a high cost.

There are sicknesses of the soul that can be specifically traced back to the harried and disenchanted conditions of advanced civilisation. We may, for example, find it ever harder to achieve inner stillness and the kind of contemplative calm required to sleep or think well. Our technology informs us of unceasing crises and opportunities to which we apparently need to be apprised on a minute-by-minute basis. There is continuously something new to consume, envy or panic about. Our own company feels like an unappealing prospect besides the maelstrom outside; there is little chance for our own thoughts to take root amid the informational torrent.

At the same time, the sophistication of our sciences and of our machines cuts us off from simpler pursuits and contact with our bodily selves. It can feel taboo to draw pleasure from what is naïve and uncostly. We forget the importance of the childlike. It is tempting to lead cosseted, insulated, denatured lives, denying the less subtle parts of our own minds and separating ourselves off from many of the claims of our bodies. It may have been a long time since we last dug our feet into the earth, whether literally or figuratively.

We offer a set of exercises specifically designed to counterbalance the more aggravating dynamics of modernity.

(i) Heartbeat news

One of the things that most sharply distinguishes modern from traditional society is the enormous importance of 'the new' and, by extension, the particular information source that promises to fill us in on novelty with great accuracy: 'the news'. Our news organisations constantly update us about the most dramatic events unfolding right now, which they mischievously encourage us to confuse with what it might be most productive for us to know about in the coming minutes. However, there is an easily missed but radical difference between 'novelty' and 'importance': what is new is not necessarily vital for us to hear about, and what we should really listen to might be very old news indeed. For example, what we might actually have to fill our minds with – and what would thereby legitimately merit the term 'news' – might not be another scandal in politics or last night's sporting victory, but an idea drawn from 17th-century Alaska or 12th-century Ireland.

Under the sway of the news, we underestimate the importance of what is cyclical, long buried or recurrent – even though it is, frequently, the slow or repeated patterns of experience that we need to attend to if we are to make sense of our lives.

As an antidote to the press of news, we might adopt an exercise that encourages us to focus in on a very unattended source of information: our own hearts. It took an amazingly long time for humans to discover the details of the essential, universal rhythm palpably occurring inside us at every minute. The heart may be only inches below the surface of the skin, but its functioning was not understood before the 1620s, when William Harvey published *Exercitatio Anatomica de Motu Cordis et Sanguinis in Animalibus – An Anatomical Study of the Motion of the Heart and Blood in Living Beings*. Even the orbit of Mars – some 225 million kilometres from us – had been accurately defined several decades before forensic attention turned to our hearts.

The most striking feature about our heartbeat is how constant it is; there are fluctuations depending on our levels of anxiety or exercise, but over the course of our lives, its average beat changes surprisingly little. Our own settled rhythm may be much like that of Queen Cleopatra or of Takaharu, the 96th Emperor of Japan, whose reign lasted from 1318 to 1339, or of the 18th-century Danish royal impostor Anna Sophie Magdalene Frederikke. Without realising it, we have a profoundly intimate bodily feature in common with billions of others, whom we mistakenly insist on terming 'strangers'.

This is why it can be beneficial and moving (albeit unusual) to ask to press one's head, gently, against another's upper body in order to hear the steady pumping of their hidden organ: we are encountering the most direct evidence of a shared humanity. They, like us, are tethered to the workings of a small, complex bundle of muscles, whose controlled convulsions started in the womb and will continue to the hour of their death.

We should take care to invest (at the price of a sandwich) in a basic stethoscope and regularly place it on our own hearts as an exercise in humility and patience. Our beat tells us something profound: that we are creatures of natural cycles; that we depend on organs outside of our conscious control; that it is a miracle we are alive and a tragic certainty that we will eventually die. Every minute,

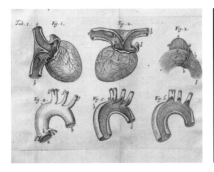 

Our curiosity had ranged far across the universe before it directed itself towards our own primary organ.

our hearts repeat the same necessary sequences. There is no progress; year on year there is (thankfully) almost no news at all from inside these chambers. It doesn't matter what is going on outside, however dramatic or fateful events seem to be; inside, the heart will be continuing on its beautifully dull, fabulously regular and awesomely painstaking work.

The sound of our heartbeat is an immediately recognisable instance of a larger fact: that we are enmeshed in bodies for which novelty is not the most interesting feature. This concept applies to our minds too: here as well, the ideas we need to take on board may not be new; the issues that we need to come to terms with may have happened many years ago, and the information that is most valuable to us may be long buried in the recesses of consciousness. A point Socrates made about democracy won't ever be a headline in the news; no bulletin is going to identify the ambiguous details of our childhood relationship with our parents; the hidden potential of our own imagination isn't going to be unlocked by the events of the last twenty-four hours.

But that is just because we are beings whose inner and true lives never move to the rhythms of the latest update. Our hearts have nothing novel to tell us – and that is precisely their point.

(ii) **Rain walking**

One of the more surprising aspects of the design of classical Japanese Zen Buddhist monasteries and homes is that they forced those who lived in them to regularly get wet and cold. In traditional examples, a key part of the house or building complex – the bathroom or the kitchen, the tea room or the bedrooms – would be separated from other well-heated living quarters by an outside walkway, usually a stone path through a moss garden, so that on many days a year, going to bed or for a wash would mean bracing oneself for a sudden plunge in temperature and maybe a light sprinkling too.

Even more surprisingly, this discomfort was not the result of an irritating design flaw or a shortfall in budget. It was a deliberate and highly respected architectural strategy carried out in the name of the wellbeing of the inhabitants. A well-thought-through house wasn't merely meant to shelter those who dwelt in it; it was – in small and calculated doses – meant to expose them to the wisdom of the elements as well.

Traditional Japanese buildings were often purposely designed to expose their inhabitants to the elements.

In Zen Buddhist philosophy, a continuous temptation of our minds is to forget that we are subject to 'nature' in the broadest sense. We tend to overlook the fact that the laws that apply to all living things apply to us too: that we must grow, flourish and then die; that little of us will remain when we are gone; that we cannot stop the forces of entropy and decay; that the universe is far mightier than we are; that any resistance must prove futile; that our time on Earth is brief and negligible. These are the lessons that we find inscribed in the life cycles of plants, in the ebb and flow of tides, in the tender cries of nightingales in spring or in river water that slowly erodes rock.

But Zen knows that our exposure to nature's lessons – and the messages of humility and acceptance that these enforce – may be severely compromised by advances in civilisation. Living in cities, benefiting from new technology, we are at risk of forgetting our fragility and exposure to primal pressures. We risk becoming proud and grandiose beings. We may sneakily start to suspect that we might be immortal and invulnerable, and our capacities for modesty as well as for generosity and sympathy for our fellow suffering beings may correspondingly wither.

This helps to explain why traditional Zen architects believed in exposing us to the elements. Shivering for a few moments on the way to the bathroom or getting wet after a dash to the kitchen, we would be reminded – in a brief but astringent way – that we remained mortal, vulnerable beings whose lives were never able to drift far from the constraints imposed on us by biology and the structure of earthly reality. Architects did not want these lessons to be delivered in a hectoring or cruel way: they took care that their walkways would be refined, that there would be a delightful playfulness in the way that irregularly shaped stones were arranged amid the plants and a pleasing degree of symmetry in interlocking, unvarnished wooden beams around which winter winds would blow. They knew too that supposedly unpleasant phenomena like 'being cold' or 'getting wet' – so long as these were framed in the right way, and connected to the deepest truths of Zen art and thought – might leave us inspired and grateful rather than resentful and humiliated. One would know that one wasn't cold because one was too silly to buy the right sort of property or had idiotically failed to insulate the corridor, but because one was an appreciative and wise student of the laws of the universe. Zen architecture's achievement was to change what a leaky walkway or draughty veranda might *mean*.

It may be too complicated and beyond our remit to relocate our bathroom to the other side of the garden, but we can all mitigate our withdrawal from the laws of the natural world. We too might choreograph a few moments when we remember – with gratitude rather than resentment – that despite our dazzling technologies, we haven't escaped the gravitational pull of nature's edicts: that we too are mortal; that we remain animals rather than robot-assisted gods; that we are subject to the life cycle no less than rabbits or cherry blossoms.

Fig. 8
Rain walking

One of the better ways to keep this in mind is through an exercise that asks us deliberately to leave the house without an umbrella, not because we are scatty, but because we are – in a metaphysical sense – focused on essential truths. Through such an omission, we can guarantee that every few months (probably not more), we will get a thorough soaking. On the way back from the station or the shops, nature will inundate us without mercy.

The standard response to this would be to scowl, to curse ourselves for our forgetfulness and to look out for someone else to blame. But as grateful participants in a rain-walking exercise, we can, like Zen Buddhists, alter what getting soaked means to us. We can almost enjoy the rivulets of rain tracing a meandering path down our necks and the build-up of a squelchy pool inside our shoes. No longer must rain be a humiliation, one more example of our idiocy; it can be an elegantly delivered reminder of the forces of nature, to which we should submit, no longer with anger and defiance, but with curiosity, grace and good humour.

(iii) Earthbathing

During our earliest months on the planet, we have no option but to spend most of our time flat on our backs, hardly able to move our heads, hoping someone will have mercy and pick us up for a look around. But once we can get going of our own accord, we tend to spring up and stay up; our waking hours are overwhelmingly spent in upright poses, with our gaze largely horizontal. We sit in chairs at meetings, jog around athletics tracks, deliver lectures from podiums, run to appointments and occasionally cross continents at high altitude. Something we rarely do is go outside at night and stretch ourselves out somewhere in a park or a field, arms and legs spread-eagled, in direct contact with the Earth, looking up, lying still, not saying very much, contemplating the sky for ten minutes or more.

There are many good reasons why we might avoid doing any of this. For a start, it looks strange; people might wonder why we don't have anything more productive to do. Then it's hard to get the temperature right. At many latitudes there are not many days a year when night-time earthbathing might be possible. But mostly, the activity feels profoundly at odds with our sense of priorities as dictated by the tempo of modern life.

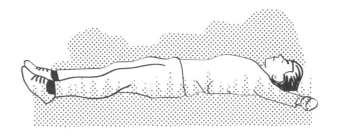

Fig. 9
Earthbathing

And yet an earthbathe might be a crucial occasion on which we recover a degree of inner equilibrium and correct some of the distorting forces of society. Carried out properly, touching the still slightly clammy soil with our fingers and tickling the grass with our heels, what should emerge most powerfully is just how small a thing we are in a vast and indifferent cosmos. Below us will be millions of near-microscopic worms and associated bacteria, waiting for us to succumb and be reabsorbed into the soil and the life cycle. Around us in the mysterious foliage might be birds – perhaps migrated from the wetlands of Algeria or the nesting grounds of southern Peru – and in the grass, bugs that might intrepidly venture across our necks or throw down a gelatinous trail across our ankles. Above us will be a mere sixty miles or so of atmosphere, before we enter a zone of unfeasible cold, in one corner punctuated by the lights of the distant Andromeda Galaxy, a dotted spiral 2.5 million light years away that started to take shape ten billion years ago.

Much of our unhappiness stems from a sense of our smallness and powerlessness in a human world in which we long to have, but are denied, sufficient esteem and control. We curse others who have failed to respect us, who do not appreciate our talents, for whom our potential is nothing, and we crave that our ego might occupy a larger space than it does. But an earthbathe pulls us in a quite different and more liveable direction. It bids us to accept our utter nullity in the grander scheme. It points us to the total unimportance of projects and resentments that otherwise occupy so much of our attention. It must matter little, under the lights of Andromeda, what we said to a colleague or who has failed to answer our calls.

Far from crushing us, this impression of the vastness of space and time in which we dwell redeems and lightens us. We recognise how many of our woes stem from rejecting our nature as insignificant fireflies and from our stubborn insistence on a status we can never securely possess.

The consolations of the Andromeda Galaxy.

Earthbathing delivers its message with elegance and kindness. It doesn't dismiss us like a waiter in a smart restaurant or an envious rival in the workplace. It tells us with nobility that we are puny and absurd. It makes us feel insignificant in a way that is oddly pleasurable. The familiar irritants of daily life seem a good deal less important from our odd vantage point. A parking ticket (which can ruin a day and preoccupy our mind for hours as we define precisely the injustice the world has visited upon us) is irrelevant; a quibble about where to go for dinner no longer feels important; an annoying work log-jam seems almost comical.

We can be a little melancholy. Almost nothing will go entirely well; we can expect frustration, misunderstanding, misfortune and rebuffs. Melancholy is not fury or bitterness; it is a gentler species of sadness that arises when we are open to the fact that disappointment lies at the heart of human experience. In our melancholy state, we can understand, dispassionately but with sympathy, that no one fully understands anyone else, that loneliness is universal and that every life has its full measure of sorrow.

But although there is a vast amount to feel sad about, we're not individually cursed and many small sweet things stand out against the darkness: love, forgiveness, creativity. With the tragedies of existence firmly in mind, we can learn how to draw the full value from what is good, whenever, wherever and in whatever doses it arises.

We are not at the centre of anything, thankfully. We are minuscule bundles of evanescent matter in an infinitesimal corner of a boundless universe. We do not count one bit in the grander scheme. This is a liberation. Rather than complaining that we are too small, we can delight in being humbled by a mighty ocean, a glacier or planet Kepler-22b, 638 light years from Earth in the constellation of Cygnus. We can gain relief from the thought of the kindly indifference of spatial infinity, where no one will notice and where the wind erodes the rocks in the space between the stars. Cosmic humility – taught to us by nature, history and the sky above us – is a blessing and a constant alternative to a life of frantic jostling, humourlessness and anxious pride.

Thanks to our feeling of smallness, we can become good and large in other dimensions. Our ego seems less impressive. We might be moved to be more tolerant and less wrapped up in our own concerns. We're reminded to focus on what is genuinely important while there is still time.

In the premodern past, religions were careful to set up a meeting with the sublime every weekend. After a week in the factory or the office or caught up in domestic life, everyone would be asked to look up at the giant ceiling of a cathedral, and there would be confronted with ideas of eternal grandeur: architecture that asserted a heritage of a thousand years and music calculated to make us feel part of the whole of humanity. But for almost everyone, that resource is no longer available. We are collectively in need of new occasions to meet cosmic grandeur in a reliable, frequent way.

One day we will be laid out in the earth forever. For now, we can lie down for a time so that our normal fretful upright lives might be a little more serene and a little less proud.

(iv) **A naked lunch**

In the summer of 1937, a group of artists, poets and their creative friends went for a picnic in the countryside just outside the little town of Mougins, near Cannes in the south of France. It was a lovely day; they ate a cold roast chicken and drank red wine. Then they all started to take their clothes off – which we know about because the photographer, model and cookery writer Lee Miller (who was sitting at the end of the table), got up and took this picture, just before full nudity unfolded. The participants weren't getting undressed because they were planning on a swim, nor were they too hot. Their nudity was a physical exercise in psychological and sexual liberation.

Lee Miller, *Picnic (Nusch Eluard, Paul Eluard, Roland Penrose, Man Ray, Ady Fidelin)*, 1937. Nakedness can be a form of psychological liberation.

They had all grown up in a world that saw clothes as central to defining civilisation, and what they were doing was casting off civilisation's intermittent burden. For almost all of human history, it has seemed obvious that what we need to do if we want to live interesting, fulfilling lives is be as civilised as possible. We have needed to emphasise order, dignity, education and technology, because only these elements separated us from the 'primitive' horrors of nature. But by the 1930s, another idea began to take shape: that perhaps we had become too civilised, that perhaps the primitive, the simple and the natural might contain something we had lost amid our cars, advertisements, suburban houses and subways. By taking their clothes off, the picnickers were, symbolically, casting off the less helpful sides of advanced society.

Pablo Picasso with his sister Lola, 1889. Unlike any other living creature, human beings in search of acceptance have long had to put on trousers, jackets, waistcoats and (often) large, lacy collars. The boy on the left is Pablo Picasso, who wasn't at the picnic that day, though he was good friends with them all. He loved the villa and the land where it had taken place – and bought it twenty years later.

Although we've missed an invitation to this particular lunch party, we can join in privately. What makes nudity so unattractive to most of us is that it's commonly expected that we should do it in front of other people. But the really important audience to our nakedness is ourselves. We should get into the occasional habit of having a naked lunch in our own company.

The prospect can be frightening. Seeing ourselves naked in bright light can make for a moment for horror: we may notice bulges we don't like, veins that are too prominent, a slightly hunched shoulder and imperfectly proportioned legs. Yet the lesson of a naked lunch is that we should dare to confront our physical selves without artifice or fear. We are forced to accept who we are: someone far from ideal but also completely normal, occasionally interesting

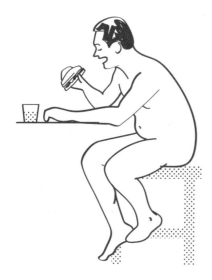

Fig. 10
Naked lunch

and, in our own way, 'good enough'. Modern society may encourage us to add ever more to our basic selves (possessions, technologies, job titles), but we are already acceptable in our primal state.

As bits of our lunch drop into our naked lap, we should smile with generosity at our bravery in carrying our vulnerable and quietly comedic bodies through a dangerous and overly serious world. We can feel the air moving in unfamiliar places – around the groin, under the armpits – and can reconnect with our beginnings, before sophistication and socialised demands began.

Our private nudity is not a declaration of war against civilisation; it is an act that redresses a balance between competing important things: recognition of our radical, metaphysical primitiveness and our immersion in the world of convention, habit and sophisticated manners.

(v) # Sun worship

In a joking tone, some of us occasionally describe ourselves as 'sun worshippers'. That can mean that we love to tan, visit an island, go to the beach, read a book, sip a drink and perhaps play some outdoor table tennis. The problem with this understanding is not that we are using too grand a term to refer to what is at heart a rather trivial and almost embarrassing enthusiasm; it's that we're arguably making far too little of, and neglecting properly to ritualise or deepen, an orientation that should lie close to the meaning of our lives.

No matter how crowded our beaches may be, in modernity our love of the sun is for the most part a psychologically shallow and unexplored commitment. Most ancient cultures didn't merely favour a tan; they worshipped the sun in and of itself, regularly bowing before it as the most potent force in the universe, to which they owed gratitude, obedience and adoration. From their sumptuous sun temples spread out along the length of the Nile, the Egyptians paid homage to the deity Ra ('sun'), depicted in their sculpture as a falcon-headed god with a solar disc over his head. The Aztecs incanted sacred poetry to Tonatiuh, the sun god and leader of heaven, while the ancient Celts, under less rewarding skies, expressed piety to Grannus, god both of the sun and, appropriately enough, wisdom.

Science has taught us too much about the constituents of our distant hydrogen and helium explosion for us to be able to deify the sun in literal terms. But this star can still occupy a place in our symbolic pantheon, where it may hold pride of place as the supreme emblem of something that no life can subsist for long without: *hope*.

Most of us have only a tenuous hold on our sources of hope. Despair stalks us relentlessly, especially in the darkness of the early hours. We are only ever a few bits of bad news away from collapse. On many days there seem so many reasons to give up and surrender to self-loathing and despondency. This is why the sun is not merely nice; it is an ally in our mind's constant attempts to structure arguments for why life might, after all, be worth enduring. Maybe there can be an end to the anxiety. Perhaps the project will work out eventually. The fights might stop. Our enemies could get bored and turn elsewhere. Our reputation might recover. A lot of things could, in the end, be more or less OK – bearable, even. The sun seems to reward such mental explorations and generously bolster them. It cannot be a coincidence that when they first draw the sun, children all over the world instinctively add in a smile.

In modernity we suffer from a reluctance to put our faith in something that we can't command and for which we must wait long periods, sometimes with great pain. Gratitude for the sun belongs to a category of satisfaction that can feel humiliatingly simple. It's tempting to deny this star's significance altogether and to focus instead on more substantial political or economic issues, by which the course of our lives is apparently more obviously determined. Nothing much, surely, hangs on how often we get to close our eyes and feel the sun's rays on our faces.

The sun:
the universal symbol of hope.

Implicitly, many powerful forces in modern society seem to agree with this view; architects are particularly keen to design buildings whose windows are tinted and will never open. There are few places in a city one might go for a small moment of sun worship, and little encouragement from employers or authority figures for us to do so.

An adoration of the sun has suffered from a shortfall in prestige. One of the most popular paintings in all of Paris's museums is a portrayal of a sunny day in a north-western suburb of the capital: Claude Monet's *Poppy Field*. And yet this work has long been held in low esteem, even derision, by serious art critics, who view it as overly 'easy' and close to sentimental.

For such critics, to love pretty skies seems to mean overlooking the actual conditions of life: war, disease, poverty and political evil. But for most of us, the greatest risk we face is not complacency – few of us are likely to be

Claude Monet,
Poppy Field, 1873.

able to forget the chaos for any length of time – or sentimental naïvety; it is that we may fall into fury, despair and unshakeable depression. It is this eventuality that the sun is well suited to correct. Given the facts of life, hope is a phenomenal achievement, and the sunny days that occasionally lie behind it are bearers of their own significant wisdom.

We can begin to rehabilitate the appreciation of the sun by seeing how seriously the star has been taken by some of the grandest figures from cultural history. The Renaissance pope Julius II was one of the most significant patrons of the arts of all time, commissioning the greatest works by Raphael and Michelangelo. He was also obsessed by the sun. In 1505, he asked Donatello Bramante to design him a new palace whose central feature was an enormous curved sun trap.

Fontana della Pigna ('The Pine Cone'),
Vatican City.

To stress his intent, Julius had a huge, Ancient Roman bronze pine cone placed in the centre of the building, pine cones being highly sensitive to the sun and unable to ripen to maturity without many hours of direct exposure to its rays.

Nearly 500 years later, when the Swiss architect Le Corbusier (1887–1965) was creating the prototypical, rigorous, logical modernist house, the Villa Savoye, he devoted huge care and intelligence to designing what he christened a 'solarium' – an elegant, futuristically shaped roof garden where one could give ample expression to devotion to the sun.

Thanks to our mastery of science, we can spread warmth without needing to beg or honour the sun. Our nuclear reactors and gas-powered stations have brought furnace-like heat to Tromsø and Murmansk, Yellowknife and Anchorage. But we may sometimes wonder whether our souls can truly be nourished at the high latitudes in which we have managed to make our lives.

To compensate for our many days of gloom, we might practise bowing down to the sun, as others might pray to more familiar gods, and there recite all the reasons we might still have to hold on to hope, despite every argument for why we might give up. As we close our lids against the sun's reviving rays, we might even imagine the faintest trace of a smile, stretching for a few hundred thousand miles across the star's 5,500-degree surface – a detail chiefly observable to people under six.

Le Corbusier,
Villa Savoye and Solarium, 1930.

Introduction

At first sight, there doesn't seem to be much of a link between thinking and exercising. We're used to heavily segregating our intellectual and our physical lives. The ambitious thinker is almost expected to be puny and inept, while the person seriously devoted to bodily fitness is often assumed to be intellectually unsophisticated.

In the gym, you concentrate on your pulse rate and build your muscles. At the library, you sit almost motionless for hours, occasionally turning the pages of a book. Nowadays, the two zones seem to have nothing in common.

Such attitudes contrast sharply with those prevalent in Ancient Greece and Rome. Here it was presumed that a well-functioning mind needed the stimulus of exercise in order to produce its best works. One could not be a great thinker and spend all day immobile on a chair or bench; thought required motion. This explains why the foremost location for both exercise and mental stimulation was a space known as the gymnasium (from the Greek word *gymnós* meaning 'naked': the chosen attire for exercise at the time). In the gymnasium, discussing philosophy and the meaning of life went hand in hand with lifting weights and stretching. Trainers were philosophers. The exercise areas were like open-air seminar rooms; the local gym was also the de facto local library. It didn't occur to the Athenians that you might have to opt for either training the body or training the mind.

The Greeks were onto a radical idea: that the right kinds of movement can unlock the best potential of our thoughts. We can extend their insight and consider a few ways in which what we do with our bodies might profitably develop what we're able to do with our minds.

Shower thinking

We might suppose that the best place to think is a large silent room with a big desk and a comfortable chair. But such luxuries are not really true to the way our minds work.

The primary obstacle to good thinking is not a cramped space or stool; it is anxiety. Often the most profound thoughts we need to grapple with have a potentially disturbing character. If we were to pinpoint them accurately and become clear about their significance, there could be a risk. We might discover that some of our past cherished beliefs were not as wise as we'd supposed; we might realise that we have been wrong about something; we might have to make some significant and tricky changes to our lives.

As these potential implications start to come into view, our inner censor, motivated by a desire for calm rather than growth, gets alarmed. A vigilant part of the self becomes agitated; it distracts us, makes us feel tired or gives us a strong urge to go online. Skilfully, it confuses and muddles our train of thought. It blocks the progress we are starting to make towards ideas that, although important and interesting, also present marked threats to short-term peace.

In this context, the shower should be honoured as one of the best places on Earth in which to carry out serious reflection. Amid the crashing water and the steam, and with freedom from the regular pressures of the day, the mind is put off guard. We're not supposed to be doing much inside our heads; we're mainly occupied with trying to soap our backs and rinse our hair. So the ideas that have been half-forming at the back of our minds – about what the true purpose of our lives might be and what we should do next – keep up their steady inward pressure, but now with less to stop them reaching full consciousness. We're not meant to be thinking and so – at last – we can think freely and courageously.

This quality of sufficient but not overwhelming distraction might also be present when we're driving down the motorway or walking in a forest; when there's just enough for the managerial, timid side of the mind to be doing to keep it from interfering with our authentic and bolder inner machinations.

We fail to do good work not because we're lazy but because we're scared. The way to release ourselves from fear is to make sure there is enough to keep us away from our worries, and at the same time enough of a chance to concentrate so that we can grab our better thoughts when they dash out of the mind like furtive deer from the undergrowth.

When we become more creative about what real thinking is like and where it can happen, we learn that the real enemy of good thinking is not a small desk or an unrewarding view; it is almost always a place that heightens rather than diminishes anxiety by not keeping the mind sufficiently busy. This is a problem for which there can be few better cures than that midwife of our deeper selves: the long shower.

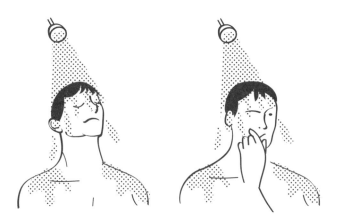

Fig. 11
Shower thinking

(ii) Window thinking

We tend to reproach ourselves for staring out of the window. We are supposed to be working, or studying, or ticking things off our to-do list. It can seem almost the definition of wasted time. It seems to produce nothing, to serve no purpose. We equate it with boredom, distraction and futility. The act of cupping your chin in your hands near a pane of glass and letting your eyes drift in the middle distance does not normally enjoy high prestige. We don't go around saying: 'I had a great day: the high point was staring out of the window.' But maybe in a better society, that's just the sort of thing people would say to one another.

Gustave Caillebotte,
Young Man at His Window,
1875.
Here the artist is seeking to
bring glamour and higher
status to an activity that,
for centuries, has been
condemned and denigrated
by moralists, teachers,
employers, parents – and
our own guilty consciences.

The point of staring out of a window is not to find out what is going on outside. It is, rather, an exercise in discovering the contents of our own minds. It's easy to imagine we know what we think, what we feel and what's going on in our heads, but we rarely do. There is a huge amount of what makes us who we are that circulates unexplored and unused. Its potential lies untapped. It is shy and does not emerge under the pressure of direct questioning. If we do it right, staring out the window offers a way for us to listen out for the quieter suggestions and perspectives of our deeper selves.

Plato suggested a metaphor for the mind: our ideas are like birds fluttering around in the aviary of our brains. But in order for the birds to settle, Plato understood that we needed periods of purpose-free calm. Staring out the window offers such an opportunity. We see the world going on: a patch of weeds is holding its own against the wind; a grey tower block looms through the drizzle. But we don't need to respond: we have no overarching intentions, and so the more tentative parts of ourselves have a chance to be heard, like the sound of church bells in the city once the traffic has died down at night.

The potential of daydreaming is not recognised by societies obsessed with productivity. But some of our greatest insights come when we stop trying to be purposeful and instead respect the creative potential of reverie. Window daydreaming is a strategic rebellion against the excessive demands of immediate (but ultimately insignificant) pressures in favour of the diffuse, but very serious, search for the wisdom of the unexplored deep self.

(iii) Sink thinking

There can be few better places to do serious thinking then at the kitchen sink after a huge dinner party or a long undomestic interval, when plates are piled up by the dozen, when glasses encrusted with evaporated red wine stretch around to the oven, when there are pans burnt with caramel to scour and dishes still half-filled with congealed Gruyère.

One of the basic tragedies of thinking is that we tend to encounter the more impressive and more beguiling thoughts of others only when they've arrived at a fairly polished, highly developed state. We read an interesting article and it seems as if the writer had just spontaneously come out with a coherent and relevant argument. By comparison, we have to meet our own thoughts

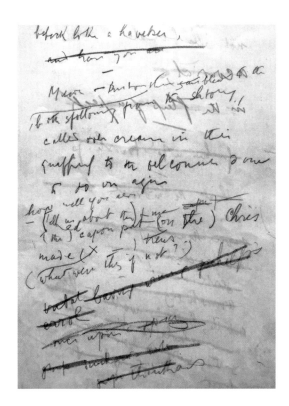

James Joyce began his challenging novel *Finnegan's Wake* with a terrible mess.

at the earliest stages of their development, when they are still muddled and confused. We compare our own stumbling, messy minds to the elegant products of others' minds and we despair. We falsely conclude that we must be idiots, unfit for any further reflection or creation, rather than that we just have a lot of tidying up to do.

Our verdict is fundamentally unfair. Others may indeed have arrived at a pointed, intelligent novel or found a neat way of explaining a thesis. But they didn't start there. Like all of us, they began with some very messy and scattered ideas. We can see this when we look at the early manuscript versions of celebrated texts. They're almost always covered in crossings out, second thoughts, arrows indicating where words should be switched round, things added in the margins, then deleted, then reinstated, then changed once again. The pages are like the mental equivalents of an extremely untidy kitchen sink.

What distinguishes these creative thinkers from the rest of us isn't where they started; it's their powers of tidying up that we should admire. Although we often associate creativity with a force that delivers its masterpieces instantaneously from a whirlwind, it is in many ways just a superior dedication to tidying something up combined with the patience required to do so.

In the modern world, washing up has a pretty degraded status. Mostly, we have no choice. We just have to stack the plates away and organise the glasses, but we see these tasks as banal impositions upon our dreams of liberation.

But it may be that wisdom lies in an opposing attitude. Physically tidying up can be a dress rehearsal for thinking. It affords us the chance to show ourselves, again and again, that disorder doesn't have to be terrifying. It isn't the end; we can, step by step, make progress. Few things go from chaos to order as smoothly and as impressively as a sink-load of washing up. However overwhelmingly chaotic the sink might look at the start, we'll gradually get all the dirt off, we'll rinse the glasses, then let things dry and put the whole lot away in less than an hour. While doing so, we will physically be going through a similar process to that involved in mental effort. We'll have to not be intimidated by the evident chaos; we'll have to break down a big job into a sequence of smaller moves; and, most importantly, we'll have to hold our nerve and not despair.

We should learn to be unsurprised by the mess inside us. Our minds are filled with divergent, ugly thoughts; our first efforts will look as if they've achieved nothing. But the experience of tidying up a sink shows us that we needn't lose hope: we'll just need to go through it bit by bit.

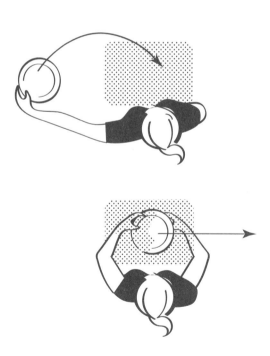

Fig. 12
Sink thinking

Rituals always have two components: there is the physical act and the meditation (or thought) that accompanies it. Without the thought, the act would often just be meaningless and strange. In Catholicism, for instance, the act of making the sign of the cross is just a very odd bodily manoeuvre if it's not accompanied by a thought of the Crucifixion: that is, of suffering endured out of love.

So too with washing up. The act gains dignity and wider resonance if we don't see it as an annoying, imposed and banal chore. We need to continually tell ourselves that this is the outward sign of a valuable inward progress. As we wipe the frying pan or rinse the bottles, we are doing exactly what Margaret Atwood or Marcel Proust did: we are tidying up.

Introduction

One of the blessings of childhood is that – if we are lucky – we can get away with spending quite a few years not thinking too much about our looks and our bodies. It isn't likely to occur to us, aged seven, to obsess over the angle of our chin or the malleability of our hair when it's so much more interesting to build a command centre in a tree or a medieval court under the kitchen table.

But such blitheness of spirit is liable to come to a sharp end in adolescence. Few of us get far past our fourteenth year without a severe crisis about our appearance. More than a concern that we are not beautiful enough (though this is generally key as well), we are likely to experience a terrifying new sense that the fast-evolving figure looking back at us in the bathroom mirror is simply not us.

We are being asked by the universe to take responsibility for a creature that doesn't accurately reflect our inner impression of ourselves. These can't possibly be our ears. We can't have eyes like that. Can that particular set of cheeks truly be 'me'? Our identity as we experience it from within comes into dispute with the blunt evidence of the mirror.

We might want to inform everyone we meet that we are not as we look. But others are in a hurry, and for 99% of those we deal with, the face ends up providing the top-line summary. For most we will be nothing more than the suggestion made by our outer envelope. It won't matter what fascinating ideas we've had, the tenderness of our heart, the richness of our imagination, the subtlety of our thoughts; we'll be our nose and awkward smile and darting eyes and little else. We have to tolerate being judged for a body that we never chose and a face we cannot easily alter. We may well inside be 'somebody else', but almost no one will ever love us enough to notice.

Unless we are especially fortunate, the existential mind-body crisis as we experience it in early adolescence never quite leaves us. We learn to accommodate ourselves to it as best we can; we resign ourselves to our wayward forehead and neck, keep encounters with a mirror to a minimum and hope that one or two saints will see past the surface to our souls.

All the while, vast industries that know our terrors only too well tempt us to try to look a little different. But given how fixed our faces are largely fated to be, we would be wiser to leave purveyors of lip gloss and conditioning shampoos aside and try another approach. We should strive not so much to alter the way we look as to alter *how* we look at ourselves – in particular, how we might do so in a more cordial and compassionate way. We are after a shift in *perception* rather than a transformation in *appearance*.

In this book to date, we have been outlining physical exercises with a power to impact the mind; now we present a set of exercises for the mind that try to shift how we view the body – in particular, how we might achieve a slightly more liveable relationship to what can feel like an unwanted impersonator.

(i) Painting one's own portrait

When we look at ourselves in the mirror, we tend not to think too much about *how* we are looking. The process feels automatic, beyond notice and immediate. It's just 'us' again: our eyes, nose, perhaps our strange ears and disappointing expression. We concentrate on what we are seeing. We don't imagine that there might be a particular way in which we are doing so, or entertain that this way might be freighted, partial, not always especially kind and amenable to fascinating degrees of change.

In order to complicate how we look at ourselves (and others in turn), we might examine the business of portrait painting. We may have no skill or particular interest in rendering a likeness of our own face on a canvas in oil paint, but during the process of appraising ourselves in the mirror, we are following in the footsteps of portrait painters, who have much to teach us about the art of living well with our own faces.

In 1871, the American artist James McNeill Whistler painted a portrait of his mother. By all evidence, she was not an especially beautiful woman.

Anna Whistler might have been inclined to view herself as haggard; she might have noted her pinched eyebrows, the bulbous end of her nose and the tendency of the muscles of her cheeks to give a sour expression to her mouth. But when looking at her for his portrait, William saw something quite different. As he worked, he was attempting to teach his mother, and the world at large, to perceive her in a more benign light.

From close up, Whistler's mother was a remarkable woman. She had grown up in a deeply traditional and conventional family in Wilmington, North Carolina. Her inherited instinct was to reject her son's bohemianism, his artistic life and his aesthetic friends, but, in fact, she warmed to them all. She put the little money she had into supporting her son's early steps as an artist, she invited

James Abbott McNeill Whistler,
Anna Whistler, c. 1850.
Whistler's mother, Anna, as she
would have seen herself in the
mirror on an ordinary day.

James Abbott McNeill Whistler,
Arrangement in Grey and Black No. 1, 1871.
What Whistler could see: the softness of his mother's cheeks,
the steadiness of her eyes, the subtle sense that she might listen
carefully when people talked to her and her refined sense of
colour coordination.

his friends to dinner and she became a much-loved and inspirational mother figure to a generation of bohemians, visionaries and social misfits who helped transform the tenor of late Victorian life.

A great portrait doesn't flatter us; instead it tells us the kinder truths about ourselves that, for multiple reasons, we have been too slow or unable to acknowledge. Our culture has taught us to assume that the normal human condition is one of vanity and exaggerated self-regard. But for many of us the opposite is true: we suffer from an excessively self-critical vision of who we might be; we are achingly alive to our defects and to all that others could perceive as wrong with our characters. A good portrait should be an antidote to the ravages of self-hatred. When we look at our faces, we should seek to become our own more kindly portraitists and to develop the humanity to find in our faces the sweeter, more engaging traces of our better natures.

We should regularly stand before the mirror and look at ourselves as through the eyes of an artist like Whistler. We're not trying to paint like him; we're trying to see like him. We can't pretend we don't have defects, but there is room to internalise a more generous and perceptive vision. We're not just what we don't like; we are also a touch of sweetness around our mouth, a look of wistfulness about our eyes, an intelligent ruefulness in the lines on our forehead and a deep bathos and humanity in our double chin.

Looking is an active process. When we say that a portrait is good, we don't so much mean that it is technically faithful. We mean that its creator has taken the trouble to find out who the sitter is and to animate their face with their soul. This isn't about faking someone's appearance; it's about creating an alternative to an impression hastily thrown up by indifference. There is never just one portrait or likeness of anyone (the history of art proves as much), whatever the extent to which we insist otherwise when, in despair in the bathroom, we label ourselves as unsightly or misshapen. We contain dozens, even hundreds, of versions of 'us'. Seeing isn't one act guided by indisputable evidence; it is a decision – one too often guided by cruelty and self-suspicion. Deciding who we are, and how we might audit ourselves, is a matter of choosing among multiple options rather than being impelled by a canon of 'facts'.

A great portrait painter isn't someone who can render a likeness; it is someone whom we admire for making an interesting and equitable set of choices, who has explored someone's nature with kindly imagination, or, as we might put it, who has judiciously weighed someone's soul and painted the result.

The German scientist and explorer Alexander von Humboldt (1769–1859) was rather lucky in terms of his hair and chin, but the fundamental appeal of his face – as depicted by the portraitist Joseph Karl Stieler – goes beyond having regular or chiselled features. On the canvas, von Humboldt looks

Joseph Karl Stieler, *Alexander von Humboldt*, 1843. This portrait conveys a visible sweetness of character that goes far beyond the word 'handsome'.

understanding. While his standards might be high (he has the look of a kind grown-up whom one longs to please), one imagines that he would not forget the need for sympathy when meeting us. Both our merits and the less than ideal sides of ourselves would be embraced and understood. The hand would be ready to tap our forearm, the mouth to say encouraging words.

Consider too how Roger Fry looked at his friend and fellow Bloomsbury Circle member Clive Bell. By any standard measure, Bell was not a beautiful man, but he was an interesting, thoughtful, sensitive and complicated one. Guided by Fry's visual choices, we can imagine Bell to have been a consoling companion through the pains of life. He would have been a good sounding-board. He wouldn't have said things just to please us; he would have given us

Roger Eliot Fry,
Clive Bell, c. 1924.

the truth while being careful not to be cruel (it looks as if things might not always have been easy for him either). He would have been with us in spirit, commiserating, offering a shoulder to cry on – and when he laughed, it would have been with genuine mirth at the follies and paradoxes of existence.

At moments of particular loathing at our appearance, we should imagine someone looking at us and doing what Fry did when looking at Bell, Stieler when looking at von Humboldt and Whistler when looking at his mother: gazing with love in order to discover and highlight what is beautiful. That is what makes a great artist and, far more importantly, a broad-hearted human.

We have looked at ourselves for far too long through the eyes of harsh critics. We now need to learn a more interesting craft: to see ourselves as might an emotionally skilful artist, ready to be benevolently perceptive about who we actually are.

(ii) The historical weight test

We tend to feel that concepts such as 'beauty' and 'ugliness' can be objectively defined, are eternally valid and are founded on unarguable criteria. Someone is either beautiful or ugly, and there isn't much more to discuss than that. More pointedly, when we consider ourselves, we can be brutally frank: we are either fat or thin, mousy or sexy, plain or pretty. We either measure up to an objective standard or – more tragically and typically – we don't.

However, this is to overlook an intriguing fact revealed by history: judgements about who and what is considered attractive keep changing, sometimes radically. A beauty in one era can be thought entirely plain in another. One century's iconically bewitching figure may elicit only a puzzled shrug a generation later. This raises an important possibility: that we might not be so much 'ugly' or 'mousy', 'beaky' or 'fat', as ignored by the partial, hasty and unimaginative current definitions of beauty. We may have nothing more to hate than the way our own age has taught itself to see.

John Smart,
A Lady, 1782.
At last, some lovely
grey hair!

Today, for example, we expect to feel dismayed and ashamed the moment our hair begins to go grey. We are about to be exiled from the realms of acceptable appearance by natural bodily processes. We might consider a wig or have our hair dyed, but inside we cannot escape the conclusion that we have become relics. But in the 18th century, this experience was unknown. When, aged 28 or 37, people noticed a grey strand in their locks, their reaction wasn't one of horror but of relief and pride. At last they were growing up, at last they were becoming the mature and admirably experienced entities to whom their societies accorded high status. Fashionable young people couldn't wait for nature to take its course and had their hair artificially greyed so as to hasten the arrival of the kind of beauty celebrated by contemporary canons of taste.

In a similar way, wearing a wig is nowadays unmentionable; to point out that someone doesn't have their own hair sounds like an insult. But it hasn't always been so. In the 1770s, the young Mozart – like all boys of his time – dreamt of the moment when he would finally be allowed to put some curled horse-hair on his head.

To take another example, beauty at present is associated with having a joyous and cheerful manner. We think of a pert-mouthed fashion model opening the perfect present, of a toned athlete in their moment of triumph or of ambitious people laughing at the beach. But other eras have emphasised quite different demeanours: in particular, the charm of faces that look as if they have known and understood suffering. Depicted in art, these faces are often not smiling but instead look lost in thought, absorbed by their own ideas and taken up with an internal dialogue around pain and loss. They may well pull a smile if asked, but it will possibly be rather strained and brief, like a moment of sunshine between dark grey clouds. Such faces can be beautiful not despite their sadness but because of it, however curious that sounds. We feel in the presence of people who would understand our difficulties; someone around whom it would not be necessary to put up a front in the name of seeming 'normal'.

School of Verona, attributed to Giambettino Cignaroli,
detail from *Portrait of Wolfgang Amadeus Mozart at the age of 13
in Verona*, c. 1770. Mozart at 13: proud, at last, to have
his own wig.

(Left) Rogier van der Weyden, detail from *Magdalene Reading*, c. 1432;
(Right) Giovanni Bellini, detail from *Madonna and the Child between
Saints Catherine and Mary Magdalene*, c. 1490.
The beauty of sadness, emphasised in the 15th century, has been less
well remembered subsequently.

Venus of Willendorf,
from Willendorf, Austria, c. 29500 BCE.
A figure to aspire to 30,000 years ago.

Aphrodite or *Crouching Venus,*
2nd century.
Aphrodite surprised as she
bathes, 2nd-century Roman
copy of a Greek original.
This is a beauty who has not
skipped breakfast.

Given how much our longing for connection is driven by the hope of being understood, and given how much of life is tragic, it follows that the sort of people we may feel readiest to find beautiful are not those whose faces suggest they find life obvious or easy, but those who seem to be as sometimes puzzled, discomfited and saddened by it as we are; those who are alive to anxiety and catastrophe – and who may, like us, frequently feel close to tears at so much that is regretful and sad.

However, the most dominant aspect of what our age considers beautiful concerns weight. Our anxiety about whether or not we are acceptable-looking has settled on a single overwhelming and obsessive criterion: the measurement of our waists. We inhabit a cultural epoch that has opted to give stupefying moral prestige to thinness.

But the connection between thinness and good looks is an astonishingly recent invention. Prior to the 1960s, few people in human history had ever thought that having a flat stomach or minuscule thighs was a recipe for beauty.

One of the oldest representations of humans, the Venus of Willendorf, routinely emphasised qualities that would be disdained by the magazines of today. Similarly, in classical times people had no problem with a few folds around the midriff, ample thighs, sturdy wrists and flat feet.

According to classical mythology, the most beautiful women in the world were the Three Graces, the daughters of Zeus: Aglaia (radiance), Euphrosine (joy) and Thalia (flowering). When the Flemish master Peter Paul Rubens (1577–1640) painted a gathering of these women, he was confident about what kind of figures he would need to accord them in order to depict them as the most alluring females of all time. Rubens was not being insincere or coy or kind; he was simply reflecting the common sense of his age in his choice of models.

Peter Paul Rubens, *The Three Graces*, 1630–1635.
The most beautiful and perfectly proportioned women ever to have
existed, according to the tastes of the 17th century.

His *Three Graces* was immediately popular because it showed what everyone
already knew about what sexiness and beauty really looked like; the work was
just repeating a well-known truth about desire.

We may think our own notions of beautiful dimensions are eternal. But they
date, at best, to around 1962, when a young woman from suburban London,

born in 1949 as Lesley Hornby, started modelling under the nickname 'Twiggy' and became for a time the most famous model in the anglophone world. But however indisputable her charms may seem, we know that she could never have secured a slot as one of the Three Graces at any time in history before her own – which should render us thoughtful about the measurements of our own waists.

The reality is that there are always more varieties of beauty available at any one point in time than a particular society or era is willing to recognise. There are as many types of beauty as there are visions of happiness: there is tiny-waisted beauty and flat-footed beauty; sad beauty and impish beauty; chinless beauty and jowly beauty. But seldom can we 'see' more than a fraction of these possibilities.

Twiggy, with a twenty-three-inch waist, modelling for *The Mirror and Herald* in 1966.

If every era tends to be blind, it is because we have such difficulty appreciating what is before us until it has been presented to us with sufficient skill, glamour and authority. We look but do not notice. One way to think of art is as a medium that has, throughout its history, used its prestige and technical talent to open the eyes of its audiences to varieties of beauty and interest that would otherwise have been missed. Every great artist's work amounts to an attempt to stir lethargic viewers into paying proper attention to a hitherto neglected aspect of reality. Through Edward Hopper's paintings, we become attuned to the beauty of late-night diners and isolated motels. The screens of Hasegawa Tohaku stir us to see the beauty of misty mornings and pine trees through fog. Marie Cassatt teaches us to look more carefully at the bond between parents and children. Thanks to Bridget Riley, we become aware of the restful quality of repeated patterns of line and colour. With Donald Judd as our guide, we start to see beauty in a monolithic series of concrete rectangles arranged on a scrubby desert horizon.

Donald Judd,
15 Untitled Works in Concrete, 1984.
Artists teach us to see beauty where previously we had been blind.

Artists do not invent the charm of the phenomena they depict; they merely reveal a charm that was always latent but overlooked by habit and prejudice. But there are never enough artists to do the world and its inhabitants justice. There are always styles of beauty that have been missed; much that fairly deserves to be admired lies in ignorance, darkness and embarrassment, starting (perhaps) with our own appearance. We too might be languishing without anyone to alert others to our particular species of charm: small-boned beauty or bald beauty; rabbit-like beauty or kindly-old-person beauty. In our way, we are like Twiggy in the age of Rubens or a splashed-paint Rothko canvas in the controlled, serene era of Piero della Francesca.

We can't shift the history of art and of perception by ourselves, but we can notice – and draw comfort from knowing – that there is likely to be ample beauty in our features already, even if the wider world is not yet in a position to see it. We are perhaps still waiting for an advocate for our kind of beauty, just like the magisterially built person living in what is now lower Austria was before the arrival of the artist who sculpted her into the Willendorf Venus. We should in the meantime not let ourselves be judged in a provincial way, by the relatively random values that happen to predominate in our particular place at our specific time. We may not be ugly at all. We are just not among people with enough imagination to know how to look at us properly.

(iii) The sorrows of the very beautiful

Some of the pain of feeling unattractive stems from the stories we tell ourselves about those we deem beautiful. They, the blessed ones, surely do not suffer. They, the gods and goddesses of the body, must have been spared the troubles with which we wrestle. In the palaces of the beautiful, invitations must not stop arriving, the attention must be constant, the options manifold, the partners on offer superlative and the praise never-ending. However otherwise sceptical we may be, we can find it hard to conceive that anyone could be at once very beautiful and very unhappy.

This accounts for the importance of a thought experiment in which we picture some of the complexities that might attend the possession of a compelling face and body. The exercise may not change our looks, but it may make us more content about the ones we have.

The list of pains confronting the beautiful might run like this:

The risk of having no character

The risk of a very beautiful person having nothing to say is high because, ever since they were 15, they have seldom had to start a conversation. Others always had to crack the jokes and develop the ideas, just for the pleasure of seeing them smile. A silence with a beautiful person is invariably the less attractive one's fault or responsibility.

It can be hard to develop a personality when others are permanently keen to project a ready-made one onto one's features. The beautiful are fated to be told who they are far more than they are encouraged to unearth interesting identities for themselves. Regular evenings alone can do wonders for one's capacity to determine where one might want to go in life and what one might really be seeking, but these moments are hard to come by when the crowd below the balcony never disperses.

The beautiful are seldom single for longer than a few months; it's just too difficult to keep turning people down. They don't face rejection in any serious way either. Who would ever leave them? Yet it's often through difficult romantic experiences that we grow to maturity. Rebuffs force us to develop compensating resources; we become stronger, more resilient; we learn compassion. It's not the fault of the beautiful, but they can end up unimaginative and a touch spoilt.

Lack of trust

In bed, the beautiful will often wonder: 'Is it me or is it my body they want?'

They want to be loved for the whole of who they are. But their exterior is so affecting, it is at risk of overshadowing everything else; it cannot be ignored.

Intimidation of the plain

The very beautiful stand to discover that very interesting people who don't look so nice are terrified of approaching them. It can be puzzling to find that one has this effect. The beautiful person may really want to get to know the quiet, fascinating type in the corner. However, this plain being can't imagine that they'd be of interest to a god or goddess and therefore emit a hostile, defensive atmosphere that wards off any possibility of a friendly remark. In a different life, the plain and the pretty might often be friends, even lovers. Just not in this one.

Even if it's not quite what the beautiful want, it may be easiest to pair up with other beautiful types; the ensuing relationships are often quite silent.

The presumption of stupidity

People don't wait to find out. Their imaginations refuse to picture the very beautiful carefully unpicking a page of Plato or analysing the state of the Swedish economy. They like the idea of the beautiful being resolutely dim.

Surely humans can't be that attractive and understand nuclear physics. That would mean too much good fortune landing in one place. However many degrees one may have, when one is astonishing-looking, the presumption of idiocy never quite departs.

Aggression

People feel that fortune has smiled on these beauties enough already. They surely don't need anything further, like kindness or understanding.

That's why the beautiful may be on the receiving end of some remarkable cruelty. Their pains and sorrows are of no interest; their so-called 'insecurities' attract scorn; they are like the tears of an oligarch. Certain people may even feel they need actively to show these beauties that they are nothing special – though they never claimed to be.

The beautiful become targets upon which disappointed others vent their frustrations with the unfairness of life in general. They seem fair game; it's assumed that they are already far too blessed with riches to get hurt.

The increased sorrows of ageing

Their body is ideal. For now. But that's why getting older terrifies the very beautiful in particular. Yesterday they found another wrinkle. Their left knee has started creaking when they climb the stairs. They will have so much more to lose when they finally become invisible. From being so high, the regret will be so much deeper.

—

By building up our vision of the inner lives of the beautiful, we're rehumanising a strangely maligned minority. And the more imaginatively we comprehend them, the less enviable (but also the more approachable) they may become.

The very beautiful only seem to be set apart from us; in truth, a millimetre below their dazzling surfaces, they are as lonely, thoughtful, needy, generous – and banal – as the rest of us, only with a few added complexities. In the end, we do not have quite so much to envy.

(iv) **What do you love me for?**

Sometimes – and it often happens in bed – we face an acute test at the hands of a lover to whom we have pledged our affections. We are asked, with little warning and in a serious tone: 'What do you love me *for*?'

Few moments in a relationship can be as philosophical or as dangerous as this. A good answer has the power to confirm and enhance the union; a bad one could blow it apart. As we try to make headway, we recognise that we can't simply say 'everything'. We're being asked to make choices, and our love will be deemed sincere to the extent that the choices feel accurate to their recipient.

The fundamental assumption behind the enquiry is that there are better and worse things to be loved for. It isn't the brute fact that we are liked that can count; the liking has to target certain of our best characteristics as *we* define them. This in turn implies that there are parts of our minds and our bodies that feel as though they better contain our essential selves than others. We are not equally present in all parts of ourselves.

When it comes to the body, there appears to be more of 'us' in our hands than in our heels; when it comes to the mind, there is more of 'us' in our sense of humour than in our knowledge of the seven times table. If a malevolent demon were to force us to give up a bit of our minds, it might be better for the maintenance of our essential selves to surrender our ability to speak a foreign language than to wipe out our taste in music, just as it would be more bearable to suffer a change in the shape of our big toe than in the profile of our nose.

To be told that we have a 'loveable mind' may be a good start, but not much more. There are likely to be many things that this mind can do well: lay a table, drive safely down a motorway, prepare a household budget or remember geographical facts. But such talents seldom feel gratifying when singled out because of their generic nature. Someone who loved us for these skills alone would have few reasons why they might not equally well wander away and love someone else at another point – and that is the very risk we are trying to ward off and are hoping the right compliment might appease.

The skills for which it is touching to be praised are those in which some of our uniqueness can be observed – for example, the way we prepare the icing for a birthday cake, pick songs for a drive through the desert, analyse a historical novel, discuss a friend's love affair or lightly tease a frustrating colleague without ruffling their dignity. If someone has noticed such details, then he or she starts to feel like a reliable candidate to whom to get attached. Their love has become specific rather than generic. It is much more gratifying for a lover to pay us a small compliment about the deft way we are able to dislodge a relative from a sulk than to be declared a sensational human for knowing the capital of New Zealand or the way to calculate the diameter of a circle.

But, to add further complexity to our demands, it isn't enough just to be admired. We also want a true lover to feel well disposed towards our vulnerabilities. Whatever our degree of competence, we are never far from moments of fear, ignorance, humiliation, childlikeness and sadness – and it is in these moods that we long for a lover to treat us with generosity. It may be pleasant to be found impressive, but it is more reassuring to discover that we are with someone who will allow us to be sad, discomfited or weepy; who has spotted that we sometimes bite our nails and worry about work late at night. We don't want to awe a lover; we want permission to be, every now and then, at our wits' end. We want them to have sufficient faith in our powers that they can be unfrightened by our periods of fragility. We need to know that the child in us has been seen and won't appal. 'I love you for being a hero,' would be an eerie pronouncement. 'I love you for being a child,' would be equally alienating. But 'I love the sad child I occasionally glimpse in you beneath your resourceful, adult day-to-day self' comes as close as one can imagine to the epicentre of love.

Our hopes for what role our body will play in eliciting love follow a comparable pattern. Here, too, sweeping generic praise feels like the work of someone who might not notice if our body were replaced by that of another in the night. It might be true that we have 'lovely eyes' or 'soft hair', but exactly the same words could be said with accuracy to millions of others.

Some of the best kinds of praise about the body are psychophysical – that is, they praise a physical aspect in order to highlight a psychological quality. They reassure us that our physical envelopes have been connected with the most loveable sides of our personalities. A perceptive lover might say:

I like the way your smile is slightly different on each side of your mouth. One side is warm and welcoming; the other is thoughtful and melancholy. You're not merely smiling; it seems as though you're thinking deeply as you smile.

Or: There is a charming thing you do with your eyelids when you are listening, half bringing them down in a quizzical way. It feels as if you're saying, 'I don't totally believe you,' but it's really an encouragement. There's an invitation, as if you were adding: 'but come on, give me the real truth; I know you're holding back the best bits because you worry you won't be understood, but you will be. You're safe with me.'

Or: There's this great thing you do with your thumb and middle finger when you get excited by an idea. It's as if you're feeling the quality of a piece of silk; as if you're touching a thought with your fingers.

Or: I'm slightly in love with the freckle on your upper left arm. It's a bit like you, quietly saying, 'Here I am, I'm me; nothing special, but I'm happy with who I am.' It's poised and unshowy but confident of its power to attract those who get it. I love that it was there when you were little and that it's been with you every day since.

In caricature, an artist looks closely at the face and body of a politician and then carefully picks out details whose exaggeration induces us to hate and mock them forever. The caricaturist will spot a slightly haughty jump at the end of the nose, a pair of unusually suspicious-seeming eyes or a pretentiously wavy curl of hair. They will then place such emphasis on these details that we will never be able to look past them again, nor cease despising the unfortunate politicians who possess them. One way to think of love is as a comparable but compassionate version of this process, whereby the lover studies their beloved minutely and latches on to elements – an index finger, the inside of a knee, a shoulder-blade or a way of closing the eyes – that become the touchstones of affection, part of the many apparently tiny but in reality sound reasons why one person has come to admire and love another.

We can add that, just as with the mind, it is frequently vulnerability in these bodily details that charms. It is the little toe and the little finger that seduce us more than the thighs or the thorax. It is the hand that curls up as it must have done in childhood that moves us. It is the thin nape of the neck normally hidden behind a confident mane of hair. It is a delicate wrist through which runs a set of intricate greenish veins. Within an otherwise mature body, we are seeing hints of an endearing, more fragile, earlier self, to whom we offer our sympathy, protection and reassurance.

The question of what we have found to love in someone should not frighten us. We need to give ourselves the time to trace back our enthusiasms to their authentic sources, while remembering that love is liable to collect with particular intensity in the most vulnerable and improbably small nooks of the self.

(v) I am not my body

A characteristic emotion on seeing a favourite novel turned into a film is puzzlement. We may not hate the actor playing a particular role – we might find them rather beautiful – it's just that they tend not to be as we imagined they should be. We never thought that Tolstoy's Anna Karenina or Kazuo Ishiguro's Stevens or Jane Austen's Marianne Dashwood or F. Scott Fitzgerald's Gatsby would look quite ... like *that*!

Beautiful perhaps – but are they really supposed to look like that? Keira Knightley in *Anna Karenina* (2012) and Leonardo di Caprio in *The Great Gatsby* (2013).

When we originally read the novel, we didn't have any fixed idea of what they would look like. Their identity was free of the tyrannical requirement of a face. We were liberated to 'see' them in their unbounded entirety, because we did not have to visualise them concretely. Their appearances were fluid and, where necessary, hazy, so as better to allow their multiplicity to take form. By not having to look a certain way, they could be far more than just one thing.

The discomfort we feel at the cinema reflects, on a small scale, the pain we are likely to experience with far greater force closer to home, in the bathroom mirror, in relation to ourselves. Here too we are prone to looking at the face in front of us and thinking – even if we do not hate how we look, though we probably do – that our features are extremely unfaithful to how it feels to be us. As with a character in a novel, we know ourselves in the comforting darkness of the inner mind, where we don't place strict boundaries or blunt conclusions on who we might be. We give ourselves latitude. We know we have a thousand moods; that we are a bewildering mixture of the kind and the selfish, the immoral and the good, the confused and the clear-eyed. We know that we harbour infinite possibilities; that we are at once artists, ploughmen, accountants, babies, presidents, lunatics, men, boys, girls, women, dolphins, okapis, jellyfish and ballerinas. Pretty much any life form that has ever bubbled up and breathed on the Earth has some echo inside us. How perplexing, therefore, to have to look in the mirror and be presented with just one particular person, with one predominant expression, one rather serious nose, one set of sensible ears and one pair of cautious lips.

This perplexing feeling first descends in adolescence. If we are frequently to be found dazed on the sofa at that age, or snappy towards our parents, or melancholic in a shapeless black tunic, it is hardly a surprise given that we have recently – and probably for the first time – become aware of how our bodies look to others, and what a cage we are condemned to inhabit, having once blithely assumed that we might be as free of definition as a cloud or an ellipsis. Our face in the mirror may come as no less of a surprise to us than would, to a reader, the arrival of a random Hollywood star in the space of a fictional persona. Someone is playing 'us' – and we're not sure we like who has been cast.

We are sometimes given advice on how to cope at this point. We must learn to love what has happened to us and who, equipped with this new body, we have turned out to be. We should consider ourselves with enthusiasm and gratitude and interpret our bodies as a gift of nature. We are, whatever we feel, *beautiful*. We should give ourselves a hug.

The advice is well meaning and in its place apt. But there might be another, starker, philosophy to try out too, this one based not so much on grateful self-acceptance as on permanently outraged but ultimately joyful and triumphant bodily self-rejection. We might look at the face in the mirror and pull an incensed, mutinous smile as if to say: *that really is not me and never will be*. Rather than attempting to overcome our initial discomfiture, we might hold on to it and make a cult of it, founding a major part of our identity on a gutsy and insolent refusal to take on board the so-called 'gift of nature' we can't stand. Following Kingsley Amis in his truculent description of his body as an 'idiot' to whom he was chained, we might consider our appearance as a banal and ridiculous actor to whom a malevolent casting agent has mysteriously decided to shackle us, and to whom we owe no particular favours or loyalty. We might think of our body as a taxi the universe has rudely shoved us into, not a vehicle we have carefully had the opportunity to choose – and to deserve.

Out of such insubordination can come a liberating lightness. No longer do we have to worry whether or not we are our own faces; we'll know for sure that we aren't. We'll hint to the world that there are armies of people, beings funnier and sadder, cleverer and simpler, more masculine and more feminine, struggling to get out. At the same time, we'll be able to bring our knowledge of the radical disconnection between outer form and inner character to bear on our views of others. We'll cease taking their appearance as any sort of truth.

We'll know that they are likely to feel as let down by their bodies as we do. We'll thereby come to 'see' beauty where no one else has learnt to spot it, because we'll be looking with new and more penetrating eyes beneath the surface. Most importantly, we'll feel compassion, for ourselves and others, for the blatant injustice of the facial lottery we have been compelled to play.

MORTALITY

Introduction

Common sense suggests that the most logical response to the idea of death should be blind terror. What more natural way could there be to relate to the anticipation of the brutal annihilation of all that we know and hold dear? How else could we conceive of an event opposed to everything that gives us purpose and direction day to day? The optimal and most mature thing we could possibly do with the thought of death should be to try to forget all about it.

Throughout the ages, artists have liked to point out that death is coming for us anyway. We might be young and apparently healthy; we might be powerful and with a lot still left to do; we might just have had a child or been invited to a ball, but death won't hesitate. Seemingly with a dark cackle, artists have produced terrifying representations of skeletal figures on horseback bearing down on us with scythes.

Gustave Doré,
Death on the Pale Horse,
1865.

They've shown us ghastly spectres who will interrupt our parties and our vain concerns with beauty and fun and pull us heedlessly down into the grave.

They've depicted fine innocent days when we feel healthy and cheerful, and reminded us that death was lurking all the while. They've even split our faces in two in order to show us that just a few millimetres beneath the radiant, fleshy surface lies a skull that will soon enough be the plaything of maggots – who will eat our lustrous eyeballs and drill corridors through our once mighty brains. We can almost hear the grim laughter down the ages.

Behind such art lies the premise that when we do finally reflect on death, the only emotions we can legitimately feel are panic and dread. Calm is not for those who really understand what is coming to them. If we are not petrified, we haven't grasped the facts. To think of death is to be profoundly terrified – a state of mind that it is the duty of the responsible artist to provoke.

Bernt Notke,
detail from *Danse Macabre*, c. 1463–1466.

This implication puts us in something of a bind. Either we keep death actively in our thoughts and should be perpetually terror-stricken, or we foolishly evade the concept and fall into vanity and naïvety. Either way we are damned.

But there might be another approach, a way of thinking a lot about death that, far from derailing and panicking us, could help to soothe and console us; a way of thinking that is at once clear-eyed and unsentimental and yet far from calamitous or gruesome. If we were to learn how to do it right, the more we thought about death, the less scared we might wind up being.

In the late 1570s, in a library in a tower in a castle in south-western France, a middle-aged, retired minor nobleman called Michel de Montaigne sat down to write an essay with one of the most seductive titles in the history of thought: 'That to Philosophise Is to Learn to Die' (*Que Philosopher C'est Apprendre à Mourir*). Montaigne had close-up experience of the terror of death. In the previous

Wax vanitas,
Europe, c. 1701–1800.

years, death had made away with his father and his best friend, and it had threatened to get him too after a bad horse-riding accident. Mournful and worried, he had fallen into depression and suffered from bad insomnia. But he was determined to overcome his fears and set his sights on using one organ above all to deal with the spectre: his mind.

He decided with unusual determination to face death down, not by denying its presence, but by marshalling extraordinary intellectual effort to defeat its chokehold over him. His essay ended up as a thorough examination of all the wisdom on dying found across the history of thought. From the Ancient Egyptians to the farmers in his locality, from the tribes of South America to his relatives and friends, he drew on every idea that made the prospect of death in any way more bearable. 'To begin depriving death of its greatest advantage over us, let us ... deprive death of its strangeness,' he wrote, 'let us frequent it, let us get used to it; let us have nothing more often in mind than death. ... A person who has learned how to die has unlearned how to be a slave.'

Montaigne's example provides us with a model and an inspiration. The idea of death is not to be avoided, but nor should it be allowed to terrify us. Our bodies are fated to succumb, but we have been blessed with minds with a particular power to interpret the end in ways that can strip it of its capacity to unsettle us. The answer to the death of the body is not denial, but the judicious exercise of the mind and, in the broad sense, of philosophy.

What follows is a series of varied arguments, long and short, practical and theoretical, playful and stern, that may allow us to walk with slightly less consternation down to the valley of death.

Premeditation

The authorities on this subject have always been clear: above all else, we must be prepared. This was the point made with particular force by the Stoic philosophers of Ancient Greece and Rome. There is plenty in our lives that we do not wish for, but – these sages advised – we are always better off if we have factored a disaster into our thinking than if we let it surprise us at a time and in a manner of its choosing. We must rob death of its power to shock us by becoming familiar with its ways and strategies; we must attend funerals, visit hospices, interview the ailing, talk to doctors, watch dissections and read anatomy books, all in order to strip death of its foreignness, in which lies – arguably – the greatest share of its power to scare us.

The Roman Stoic philosopher Seneca suggested a method for what he termed in Latin a *premeditatio* (a premeditation), whereby we should carve out a little time every day (Seneca recommended the early morning) in which to imagine the very worst that could happen to us or those we love in the hours ahead. Every day we should reflect exhaustively on all mortal eventualities: we might fall down the stairs; a stranger might stab us; a loose tile could finish us off; a disease might destroy us; our child could choke on a fish-bone. We should never think that death might be unfair or mysterious. Its monstrous power over us should be understood and continuously rehearsed. Seneca shared his own morning premeditation:

[The wise] will start each day with the thought ... Fortune gives us nothing which we can really own. Nothing, whether public or private, is stable; the destinies of men, no less than those of cities, are in a whirl. Whatever structure has been reared by a long sequence of years, at the cost of great toil and through the great kindness of the gods, is scattered and dispersed in a single day. No, he who has said 'a day' has granted too long a postponement to swift misfortune; an hour, an instant of time, suffices for the overthrow of empires. How often have cities in Asia, how often in Achaia, been laid low by a single shock of earthquake? How many towns in Syria, how many in Macedonia, have been swallowed up? How often

has devastation laid Cyprus in ruins? We live in the middle of things which have all been destined to die. Mortal have you been born, to mortals have you given birth. Reckon on everything, expect everything.

With such lucid realism, we were to face the day with neither dread nor meekness. The Stoics knew that, by not thinking about death, we can never manage to escape its power over us. The fear is still there; it's just dispersed, unself-aware and hence corrosive. It seeps out, metastasizes and starts to infect every corner of our lives. It shows up as megalomania or rage, sexual addiction or alcoholism, panic attacks or hypochondria. We end up scared of everything because we have forgotten that there is one very large thing we are carefully omitting to think about.

Once it's been examined by our full powers of reason, most of what worries us can be drained of its unsettling qualities. To do this properly, we need to surrender the sentimental optimism with which modern society cruelly imbues us and associates with health and courage. We should settle into a mood of defiant tragic realism laced with humour and kindness. We should turn over in our minds just how we could cope if the worst were to come to the worst, and know that we would discover extraordinary resources in ourselves to cross the door through which hundreds of millions have gone before us.

When the fatal verdict is given to us, we will cry and rage and think it madness and an absurdity before gradually accepting it as the necessity it is. We will retreat to bed and, under the protection of the covers, weep uncontrollably for days, no longer holding back, riding every wave of grief until we can sob no more. Then we will discover that what may make life worthwhile is not how long it is but how intensely and gratefully one has lived it. We will feel emboldened to reach out to others in our position and share stories of confusion without pride and face the terror in company. We will learn to contemplate our end from a higher vantage point and at moments, in a consoling way, recognise our lives as the petty and insignificant things they truly are and always were. We will prepare to rejoin the eternity of silence from which every life is only ever a brief interruption. Then, one day, the rage, grief, anxiety and fear will be at an end, and we will, at last, as the prayers so beautifully put it, be at peace.

A more death-ready society would mention the idea of dying so often it would allow us the greatest victory over it: to get bored at its very mention. Death would be the ultimate 'old story', with nothing interesting to tell us and no power to shock us. We wouldn't so much as shudder when it finally rang or hammered urgently at our door; we would have been anticipating and preparing for the call all our lives.

(ii) ## Scepticism

The reason why it is so easy to forget death – and therefore to end up so terrified by its unexpected arrival – is that, for many years, it keeps itself skilfully off-stage. For decades, we are allowed to feel that our body is under our command. It seems to do whatever we want; it proceeds flawlessly through the challenges we present to it. It doesn't do more than let off an occasional sweet gurgle. It says nothing of what's happening inside; it gets on with the task like an efficient and uncomplaining robot. Along the way, we're encouraged to believe that we can control this body – possibly forever – by strict adherence to medical and dietary regimes. If we eat kale, take 10,000 steps a day and work out five times a week, then perhaps the rumours might have been wrong all along.

But a wiser approach is to remain profoundly sceptical of the body. It may appear to be our friend and reliable carrier; it may seem to obey the laws of health; but it is and does no such thing. It is a complicated, fragile, peculiar, erratic and in the long term desperately dangerous machine over which we have very little control and not much understanding. We have been tethered to a slowly dying animal with a will of its own, and that reserves a thorough indifference towards the books we like to read, the love affairs we seek to conduct, the children we still have to bring up and our hopes for the future of humanity.

To bring the message home, we might learn to take a particular interest in our X-rays.

Although we may in theory be aware of our substructure, it is still strange – and a rare, unnerving modern privilege – to glimpse right through the flesh of our own arm or hand. It is like being suddenly introduced to a set of people who have been living in a secret cavity of our own house for years. We meet the distal phalanges and metacarpals of our fingers that are always only millimetres from our sights; bizarre, hardened, calcified struts and protuberances that have

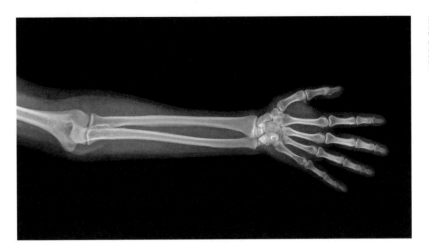

Getting better acquainted with our
unfamiliar and fragile bodies.

enabled us to stroke our partner's hair, wipe away our tears, type our memoir
and point to a transcendent sunset on a Greek island, but to which we have
seldom ever given a thought and couldn't reliably pick out in a line-up of the
X-rayed forearms of a group of strangers.

We're an eternally odd amalgam: a core of rigid parts, coated in pulpy, flexible,
tender flesh packed with mysterious pipes and sacs of chemicals; a mixture of
the solid and the soft, of strength and delicacy. We can haul a wardrobe up to
the second floor or make a minutely accurate drawing of a leaf; we can plan
the next hundred years or die tonight slipping on a bar of soap in the shower.

One message of the X-ray is about our kinship with other living things. To
our normal perception, we don't look remotely like a seal, whose life cycle we
might pity and shudder at.

Although we appear to have little in common with a creature that spends its life
swimming in cold coastal waters, diving for herring and flounder and basking
on rocks, the deeper probing of the X-ray suggests otherwise.

A common seal basking on a rock,
Lismore, Scotland.

Perhaps not so different after all.

For nature, seals are our cousins, with comparable rib-cages, front paws, feet and skulls – and bodies that are, like ours, constrained by biology and destined to die with bathos and a raucous groan. We may already know, in theory, that we share an evolutionary ancestry with the wider animal realm, but we too often confuse ourselves with our machines and our buildings, our philosophies and our projects, though we are never far from the destiny of beasts and our lives will be no less hard, absurd and brief than theirs.

(iii) Gallows humour

The traditional mood that surrounds death is solemnity. We speak of this calamity in respectful whispers; at its mere mention, we adopt a reverential tone and put aside all the mirth and irony that we normally use to defend ourselves against the humiliations of life, in order to become prim and unsmiling cardboard versions of ourselves. There are few remarks as arid, timid and portentous as those that otherwise normal and witty people find themselves uttering to the families of the bereaved at a funeral.

However, exercising this sort of humourlessness is to give death too much of an advantage. Why should death strip us of our capacity to laugh? To laugh at death is not to overlook its seriousness or power; it is to refuse to let these defeat us. It is to remain sensitive to the absurdity of having to be thrown off the planet by something as daft as an impediment in the internal carotid artery of the brain or a malfunctioning tricuspid valve in the chambers of the heart.

We can fall prey to a superstition that, by not mentioning loathsome facts, we may somehow skirt them. But not mentioning death is to give it an undue authority over us. We should mock it to the degree that it attempts to petrify us. In the Middle Ages, a tradition arose of condemned people on the scaffold turning to the crowd and making a witticism about their situation – the birth of so-called 'gallows humour'. Freud recounts a man being led out to be hanged at dawn saying, 'Well, the day is certainly starting well.' One aristocrat in the French revolution, on being ushered up to the guillotine (then a brand-new, high-tech killing machine), looked up at its complicated workings and asked, 'Are you sure this is safe?'

Gallows humour is unsqueamish about looking bleakness straight in the eye. Rather than being slowly gnawed at by sideways glances, the gallows humorist faces disaster head on, insists they will not be silenced by it and defies it to do its worst. Our contagious laughter is a species of grateful relief at witnessing our greatest fears kicked off-stage with audacious courage.

Our bodies deserve particularly strong doses of this kind of irreverent humour. They are, from many angles, plainly ridiculous contraptions. It is a wonder that we are ever able to take ourselves seriously knowing that we're living on top of a two-metre-long colon filled with varying degrees of moist faecal matter encased in a lining likely eventually to develop a cancerous polyp that will spread to the liver and prove to be the end of us. We may be able to listen to Bach and think of Tolstoy, but we also have stools forming inside us made of bits of the potato croquette and aubergine fritter we ate for lunch. Shitting should be a daily definitive argument against the possibility of ever taking ourselves too seriously. An image of the human colon kept always close by might save us from those times when fantasies of immortality or dignity threaten to get the better of us.

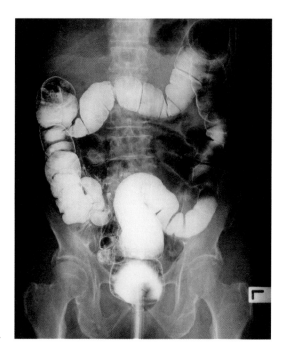

We are, in the most
profound sense, full of shit.

It is one of the many examples of the supreme wisdom of Pieter Bruegel the Elder that, in all twenty-one of his surviving paintings, we can somewhere in the frame locate a person taking a dump.

As Bruegel's literary twin Montaigne (1533–1592) wrote: 'Kings and philosophers shit, and so do ladies.'

Pieter Bruegel the Elder,
The Tower of Babel, 1563.

We should not humbly beg for mercy in front of death. There is no reprieve for good behaviour. Instead, let's remain death's unruly pupil, mocking it from the back row and the toilet seat, bidding it to come and get us if it dares and laughing defiantly in its face when it does.

(iv) In praise of siestas

One response to the troubles our bodies give us is to live as though we could rely on the mind alone. It is tempting to pretend that the body has no particular claim on us, and to overlook how much it controls who we can be, what we can achieve and how we're able to think.

We may mistakenly imagine that the ideas circulating in our minds must always be a product of reason, and rest upon intellectual foundations assembled from sober arguments. The way we feel about politics, our assessment of our professional future, our view of holidays or the manners of our children can appear to have formed in our minds on the basis of rational induction alone. But in truth, much of what is in consciousness is merely the shadow and puppet play of the body's inclinations, playing itself out in the theatre of the mind. A passing mood of optimism may come down not to our thorough or realistic evaluation of the prospects for humanity, but to the ingestion of 250 ml of orange juice; an equally strong mood of despair and fury may be founded not on genuine grievance but on a collapse in blood sodium levels.

We are especially inclined to forget the extent to which what we think has been coloured by how much we have slept. It is well understood by wise parents that the very young should only go for so long without a nap. After baby has spent a pleasant morning, after friends have come around and brought presents and made animated faces, after there has been some cake and some cuddles, after there have been a lot of bright lights and perhaps some songs too, enough is enough. Unless some urgent preventive measures are taken, baby will start to look stern and then burst into tears. The experienced parent knows that nothing is particularly wrong (though the baby may by now be wailing); it is just time for a nap. The brain needs to process, digest and divide up the welter of experiences that have been ingested, and so the curtains are drawn, baby is laid down next to the soft toys and soon it is asleep and calm descends. Everyone knows that life will be a lot more manageable in an hour.

Sadly, we exercise no such caution with ourselves. We treat our brains as if they were robust computers rather than delicate organs housed within a fickle animal that must be soothed, watered, fed and regularly allowed to rest. We schedule a week in which we will see friends every night, in which we'll do twelve meetings (three of them requiring a lot of preparation), where we'll make a quick overnight dash to another country on the Wednesday, where we'll watch three films, read fourteen newspapers, change six pairs of sheets, have five heavy meals after 8 p.m. and drink thirty coffees – and then we lament that our ideas feel scrambled and that we are close to mental collapse. We refuse to take seriously how much of our vulnerable babyhood is left inside our adult selves and, therefore, how much care we must take of our bodies if the mind is to have any chance of retaining a hold on sanity. What register as anxiety, ill temper and sadness are typically not real phenomena, but symptoms of our bodies' enraged pleas for us to put them to bed.

Hubristically, we assume that most daylight hours can sensibly be devoted to work without any ensuing cost or penalty. But the body insists otherwise. Unless we are too stubborn to hear it, it will always call out – at around three

Fig. 13
Hammock thinking

in the afternoon, in that widely known but rarely mentioned blank zone where, in organisations and offices around the world, despite a patina of activity, nothing of value has ever been thought or done – to be laid down somewhere on a bed, divan, sofa, corner armchair, field or hayloft and left to itself for twenty minutes.

The sophistication of any civilisation could be measured via a people's readiness to accept – whatever the inconvenience – a primary role for the siesta and the extent to which it can build in measures to accommodate it in its architecture, social routines and works of art.

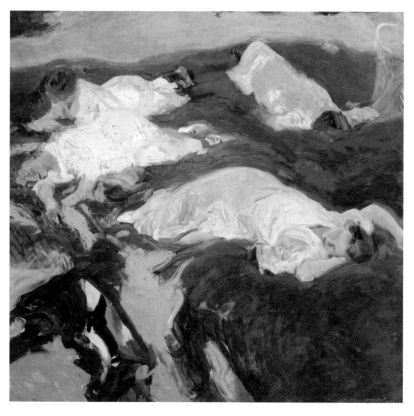

Joaquín Sorolla,
La Siesta, 1911.

The siesta symbolises a mature recognition of our fleshly reality and of the limits set by our biochemical make-up on our ability to think and act well. We are not being lazy; we're acknowledging that we are not sole masters of our house and that if we are to permit the best of ourselves to emerge, we have to do justice to our stifled yawns.

A civilisation that does not accept a role for siestas is likely to be one that can't accept a place for dying, or more generally cannot come to terms with the cap placed on human endeavour by biological reality. It is a civilisation that has not squared up to its own nature.

When we have learnt how to stop and take a nap, we are also likely to have grasped that we are mortal, and must therefore be kind enough to ourselves and others to pay heed to the wisdom of exhaustion.

(v) Bow to necessity

Because death is always such a personal tragedy, because it can sometimes feel as if it was something we have been singled out for while others are still playing volleyball down at the gym in full health, it is helpful to be reminded that it will eventually prove a non-negotiable necessity for every living thing on the planet, from the Burgundy snail to the South American tapir, from the dental hygienist to the genius-level left-side hitter.

There can be consolation in contemplating the presence of death in species and life forms other than our own, just to enforce the message of the ubiquity of the end. In a photograph by Ansel Adams, a row of aspens have

Ansel Adams, *Aspens, Dawn, Autumn, Dolores River Canyon, Colorado*, 1937. Contemplating our own mortality in the falling leaves.

been surprised by the photographer's light and stand out as strands of silver against the blackness of night. The mood is sombre but elegant. There is a consoling message within the artistry that can appease our raw grief and anxiety about our mortality and the fleetingness of time. The image invites us to see ourselves as part of the mesmerising spectacle of nature. Nature's rules apply to us as much as they do to the trees of the forest. It's not personal. The photograph is a reframing device; it invites us to think of our own deaths as having a natural order that has nothing to do with individual justice. The photograph tries to take the personal sting out of what is happening to us.

Leaves always wither and fall. Autumn necessarily follows from spring and summer. Encountering this spectacle in art, we are invited to reframe our thoughts about mortality in the broad purview of nature: nature's sequences apply to us as much as they do to plants and trees. Time moves forward relentlessly. The seasons pass and we hasten towards old age, death and oblivion. The image takes these awkward truths and, through its technical skills, lends them a redemptive dignity and grandeur.

Whatever our politics, death is the most democratic process we will ever be invited to take part in. No one escapes it, no matter their status. The best excuses won't let us off. We get a measure for what this really means by studying a picture of a vast swarm of people, perhaps on a beach in high summer, many decades ago. No one, amid the buckets and spades, the ice cream stands and the prams, the tanned skin and the flirtations, will get away with it. Every single person, however special their thoughts and individual their circumstances, will have to go (or has already gone) down the same path.

Think of 10,000 people gathered on a beach for some high summer fun. To us, now, it looks like an age of innocence, but even then, death was working its way through the crowd – quietly, deftly, but inexorably. Certainly, these deaths were mourned, but for most there were no flames, no explosions, no headlines, no widespread outpourings – it was too dispersed.

It can be helpful to consider
an image of a teeming mass
of people such as this and
contemplate how every single
human here is destined to die;
no one escapes the final end.

And yet each death was nonetheless a catastrophe, with the same wrenching story of unfair loss, the same hopes suddenly quashed, so many individual stories following one ineluctable script; some stories beginning with a cough in the bathroom, others with a sore knee at work, a few with a lump being examined in the surgery, but all ending up in exactly the same place. Montaigne summed it up well: 'When Socrates was told that the Thirty Tyrants had condemned him to death, he retorted, "*And nature them!*"'

(vi) Living deeply

History is filled with stories of extraordinary figures who died tragically young: John Keats (26), Emily Brontë (30), Alexander the Great (33), Mozart (35), Sylvia Plath (30), Van Gogh (37). In *The Death of Géricault*, the brilliant Romantic artist – who a few years before had won international renown for his painting *Raft of the Medusa* – is shown stretched out on his bed in his Parisian studio in the Rue des Martyrs, having just succumbed to a typhoid infection developed after a riding accident; he was 33 years old.

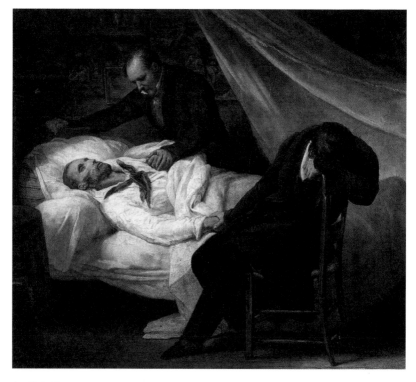

Ary Scheffer,
The Death of Géricault, 1824.
Many people of extraordinary talent
have died young; perhaps it is best to
try to live deeply than to live long.

Given the extent of their contributions, it seems appalling how young these talents died. But when we zero in on the oft-remarked detail that they seem to have achieved more in a few brief years than many of us achieve in eight decades, a new thought opens up. The very discrepancy between us and them suggests that we are perhaps overly blunt when we measure lifespan in a unitary way, without reference to what someone is doing with the years they have been allotted. A year in the hands of a person who is open to experience, who creates, feels, loves, connects and delights, is a lot 'denser' and in that way *longer* than exactly the same amount of time in the hands of a less responsive and less inwardly generous human being.

We might go so far as to propose that a year in the life of the former should be given a different numerical weight than one in the latter – that a year in the life of Géricault or Emily Brontë should not be counted in exactly the same way as a year for someone else, and might more rightly be doubled or more. We know in travel that two days in a particularly vibrant city can feel like a year in another, less inspired place. The same is true of life more broadly; not everyone who is living is equally alive. Just as we calculate dog years to take animal size and anatomy into account, so we might recalibrate lifespan according to the depths of meaning one has plumbed, not the gross years one has breathed. Adjusted for the intensity of experience, we might hence judge that – whatever basic chronology might claim – Mozart really died at around 120, Sylvia Plath at 80 and Géricault in his mid-70s.

All this matters because our sadness at the idea of death frequently reduces itself to the thought that our lives have not been, as we put it, 'long enough'. But we shouldn't measure a life by the hours it contains; rather by the wisdom, love and intelligence with which these hours have been spent. By that score, many of the people most legendary for having had brief lives really had nothing of the sort.

It doesn't matter if we have no genius-level capacities at poetry or painting; it still remains for us to choose how purposefully and beautifully and therefore ultimately how 'long' we can live. We should not stay transfixed, or devastated, by the simple number of days liable to be ahead of us; we should concentrate on how to sprinkle them with meaning.

There is a powerful death scene in Giuseppe Tomasi di Lampedusa's novel *The Leopard* (1958). The elderly Fabrizio Corbera, Prince of Salina, who is the psychological centre of the book, is about to die. He's lying in bed with his weeping relatives around him. And he asks himself the terrifying, fundamental question: *how much of my life have I actually lived?* The answer is disturbing: he can pick out a few months here and there – two weeks before his wedding, two weeks after; a few days around the birth of his first son; certain hours he spent in his observatory (he is a distinguished astronomer); a few hours of flirtation here and there; times when he was reading aloud to his children; conversations with one or two friends, particularly his nephew. But not much in total: perhaps a year or two out of seventy. If we measure the reality of our lives by the quantity of time we have passed in a state of genuine happiness, the answer is going to be distressing. But it might be the right way of sizing up the length of a life. We should be more focused on how well we have lived rather than the absolute number of days we have existed.

In the end, we are not short of time. What we're truly short of is affection, open-heartedness, kindness and tolerance. We're short of the ability to create peak experiences in which we are sufficiently unfrightened, approachable and responsive. We may have a lot to mourn, but it isn't necessarily the imminence of death; it may be the difficulty of living with courage and sensitivity. The challenge of our lives is to learn to live deeply rather than extensively.

The artist John Isaacs depicts a ravaged corpse in a gallery; its stomach hangs out, its ribcage appears to have been hacked at like a butcher's carcass. But the real horror and rebuke lies in the title of the work: *Are you still mad at me?* The tone is calculatedly banal next to the ghoulish fate that has befallen what we take to be someone's erstwhile partner. The poor corpse before us might only a little while ago have spent their time in an apartment, squabbling with their loved one, certain they were right but not being able to see things through another's eyes. And now their pettiness is being judged from the perspective of death. Are we really to spend the only lives we will ever know in yet another argument about who disrespected whom, when outside the narrow cavern

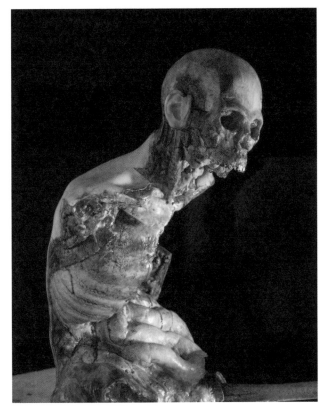

John Isaacs,
Are You Still Mad at Me?, 2001.
This deliberately ghoulish artwork
might help us recalibrate our notions
of what is really important in life.

of our embittered relationship, so many opportunities for joy and wonder remain? Are we going to walk towards death without properly filling our lungs with the beauty of existence? We aren't here being warned that we're going to die – that is eminently survivable as a thought; we are being warned of a far more appalling but less often mentioned danger: that we might die *in the midst of a sulk about not very much.*

We can't command how long we live, but it is very much in our remit to try to adjust how colourfully and how deeply we live. We may have to rethink what a 'premature' death actually is. It isn't necessarily what happens to a young artist gone by 30. In a fairer assessment, he or she may have been a nonagenarian or more. Even if we are well past middle age, it is we who might be heading for a regrettably 'early' death. Our goal should not be to lay claim to yet more decades; it is to ensure that we do everything in the days ahead to learn the art of appreciation.

(vii) The ultimate escape hatch

One reason why we fear death so intensely is that we imagine it in devastating contrast to the life we lead now. We compare a hideous end with our current relatively blessed circumstances. We align the thought of death with the joys of conversation, with travel, children, friends, long, hot baths and quiet evenings at home with books. No wonder we quickly fill with immense regret. Next to what we have now, death seems to entail unbearable loss.

But what we are forgetting is that for the vast majority of us, by the time we are close to death, the sort of life we will be leading will have little in common with the one we have now. We won't be able to make it up the stairs, we'll regularly wet ourselves, we'll have a continuous pain in our backs and in our lower legs, we'll hardly hear anything – and there'll be a constant dribble flowing from our toothless mouths. Our minds will only show brief flashes of awareness against a dim, somnolent night; it will be hard to remember who of our friends is alive (most won't be), where we have lived, how many children we have had or quite who we are. The energetic, focused, pleasure-seeking self we currently inhabit will be as remote from us at that moment as we are now from the confused, semi-conscious months of early childhood. In other words, there will be a lot less to lose. We should not pre-emptively regret a richness in life that will almost certainly no longer be ours.

What is more, were we to be in terrible pain, we would not have to continue. It was a key tenet of Stoic philosophy that we could free ourselves from a debilitating fear of death with the thought that no pain ever has to last very long, for we have all been granted the ultimate escape hatch. Two thousand years of Christian heritage has made support for this approach feel shocking, but it is not necessarily unwise. The Stoics associated happiness with dignity, with a state in which we were not to be held hostage by any malevolent force, but they understood that this dignity could be lost if, for example, certain sorts of illness assailed us and tortured us minute by minute. At that point, they recommended that we be allowed to regain our freedom without compunction. We were to try to live well for as long as possible, but not insist on continuing costs when matters had come to an unfeasible pitch. As Seneca put it:

The wise man will live as long as he ought, not as long as he can. ... He always reflects concerning the quality, and not the quantity, of his life. As soon as there are numerous events in his life that give him trouble and disturb his peace of mind, he sets himself free. ... He holds that it makes no difference to him whether his taking-off be natural or self-inflicted, whether it comes later or earlier. He does not regard it with fear, as if it were a great loss; for no man can lose very much when but a driblet remains. It is not a question of dying earlier or later, but of dying well or ill. And dying well means escape from the danger of living ill. ... Live, if you so desire; if not, you may return to the place whence you came. ... If you would pierce your heart, a gaping wound is not necessary – a lancet will open the way to that great freedom, and tranquillity can be purchased at the cost of a pin-prick.

Very few Stoics ended their lives prematurely (though Seneca was an exception). To make a case for a voluntary end was not an active recommendation – and there is no doubt that ending one's own life leaves a dark legacy for those left behind – it was a piece of encouraging mental insurance against pervasive worry about our later years and the pains these might bring. Knowing that we do not have to be here any longer than we wish should liberate us to enjoy a future without fear.

Under the aspect of eternity

One of the most useful things about our minds is that they can allow us to step outside of ourselves, to consider our death from a wholly dispassionate perspective, as if it were someone else who would have to go through the event and as if we could understand it in the same way that a stranger four centuries from now might. In other words, we can think of our own demise as if it might not be such a big deal – just an inevitable return to an atomic mulch from which our life was only ever a brief and unlikely spasm.

The 17th-century Dutch philosopher Baruch Spinoza made a famous distinction between two ways of looking at death. We could either see it egoistically, from our limited point of view, as he put it in Latin: *sub specie durationis* – under the aspect of time – at which point it would be a tragedy. Or we could look at it from the outside, globally and eternally, as if from the eye of another force or planet: *sub specie aeternitatis* – under the aspect of eternity – at which point it would be an untroubling and normal event. Spinoza recognised that, for much of our lives, we are necessarily pulled by our bodies towards a time-bound and egoistic view, aligning all our concerns with survival. But he stressed that our minds also give us unique access to another perspective, from which the particulars of our material identities matter far less. Our minds allow us – and here Spinoza becomes lyrical – to participate in eternal totality and to achieve peace of mind by aligning ourselves with the trajectory of the universe.

We can put Spinoza's ideas to work for us by taking a few minutes to lie on our back in bed, focusing our minds upwards and outwards. We can imagine floating free of ourselves, piercing the ceiling and the roof and rising above our district and our city, climbing until we could see the whole countryside and the coast, then the sea (plied by ferries and container ships), then the ocean, the next continent, mountain ranges, deserts, until we penetrated the outer atmosphere and entered deep space. We might continue outwards through our solar system, out into interstellar space, then intergalactic space, past 400 billion stars and 100 billion planets, past Sagittarius A and the Laniakea Supercluster and on to the furthest galaxy from Earth in the universe, MACS0647-JD, where we would finally rest, 13.3 billion light years away from our own bedroom.

When we have the courage to know it, we are staggeringly unimportant in the larger scheme. On a cosmic scale, nothing we will ever do, or fail to do, has the slightest significance. Everything connected directly to us is of no importance when imagined on an appropriate scale. We are negligible instances, inhabiting a random, unremarkable backwater of the universe, basking for an instant or two in the light of a dying star. This perspective may feel cruel, but it is also redemptive, for it frees us from the squeals of our own frightened egos. It has only ever been an illusion, and a painful one at that, to imagine that our lives have any significance. We would feel so much lighter and freer if we could only acknowledge that we are and have always been as nothing.

For much of our lives, we have no option but to exist in a state of what one might term 'lower consciousness': we respond melodramatically to insults; we cling passionately to our interests and desires; we worry intensely about the image we have in the eyes of a few hundred fellow humans we know of. However, at rare moments, when there are no threats or demands upon us, perhaps late at night or early in the morning, when our bodies and passions are comfortable and quiescent, we have the privilege of being able to access 'higher consciousness'. We loosen our hold on our own egos and ascend to a less biased perspective, casting off a little of our customary anxious self-justification and brittle pride. In such states, the mind moves beyond its particular self-interests and cravings. One can imaginatively fuse with transient or natural things: trees, the wind, a moth, clouds or waves breaking on the shore. From this point of view, status is nothing, possessions don't matter, grievances lose their urgency and not being around any more doesn't have to be a disaster. If certain people could encounter us at this point, they might be amazed at our newfound generosity and tranquillity.

States of higher consciousness are generally short-lived. But we should make the most of them when they arise, and harvest their insights for the panicky periods when we require them most. Higher consciousness is a huge triumph over the primitive mind, which cannot envisage the possibility of its non-existence. We can't know what our end will be. Maybe we'll be lingering for years, hardly able to remember who we are; maybe we'll be cut off by a horrifying internal growth, or a key organ will fail us and the end will be instantaneous. But we can imagine our funeral, the things people might say or feel they have to say; we can imagine people crying, our will being enacted, then being gradually forgotten, becoming a strange figure in a family photo. Soon enough we'll diminish into uncertainty ('One of my great-grandparents was a lawyer, I think, maybe …') and then we'll be entirely unknown, a footnote in an uninteresting record lying in an unexamined file somewhere in a never-visited archive. It will be as if we had never been.

To meditate on the unimportance of our own end, strangely, does not make it more frightening. The more inconsequential our death, the more vivid our appreciation of being alive. Our conscious existence is unveiled not as the inevitable state of things but as a strange, precious moment of grace. Wise at last to the fact that our existence is but a fleeting second, we may be filled with wonder to be here at all, and no longer quite so sad about the time when we no longer will be.

[ix] The courage of death

Until here, we have been seeing the fear of death as a problem that we could strive hard through reason to overcome. However, we should not forget the utility of this fear when it is well marshalled.

What we should sometimes strive for is not to be less afraid of dying, but to be much more afraid than we currently are, to guarantee that we have a chance of leading the sort of lives we truly deserve and that can make us who we should be.

There are so many things that we would ideally need to do right now, but that we leave aside because we are scared. We are scared to fail. We are scared to be alone and to examine our own feelings. We are scared to eject certain people from our lives even though they depress us and bring us down. We are scared to tell our partners who we really are. We are scared to take our dreams seriously. From fear, we delay the lives we know we should be leading.

There is a dark though useful solution to this delay. It does not involve reassurance or reminding ourselves that there is time. It involves focusing our thoughts on something radically scarier than any of our day-to-day doubts and hesitations; a terror that can jolt us from our timid lethargy because – beside it – there is nothing very serious to fear.

We should use the thought of death to shake us into more committedly pursuing the life we know we need to lead. We will be able to act decisively on so many of our important hopes when the fear of death is finally allowed to trump the fear of failure or humiliation, compromise or shame.

With the best of intentions, we may need to nurture the fear of death. We should consider how often cancer and heart disease strike far ahead of the average age of death. We should read of the violent and cruel ways of strokes and aneurysms. We should talk to people who have turned 60 and let them explain to us how swiftly the years went.

We should terrify ourselves, not in the name of despair, but for the sake of a more usefully impatient, courageous and authentic spirit. We should get scared about the one big thing we should fear, and thereby be liberated from the hundreds of low-level apprehensions that don't deserve any of our precious time.

[x] # The delectable life force

Let's turn – a little surprisingly – to pornography. People have been making pornography for a very long time. It's been on the sides of temples in India, on Greek vases, in Roman bedrooms and German drawing rooms.

(Top) Erotic fresco from the House of Vettii, Pompeii, Italy, c. 1st century.
(Left) Rim of an Attic red-figure kylix, from Athens, Greece, c. 510 BCE.
(Right) Peter Fendi, *The Lovers*, 19th century.

Félix-Jacques-Antoine Moulin,
Two Standing Female Nudes, c.
1850.

But a decisive moment in its history came in 1839 with the French artist Louis Daguerre's invention of the photograph, known as the daguerreotype, which transformed the availability and realism of sexual imagery. It was not long before the new technology was being put to use to explore a variety of explicit scenarios. One of the earliest – a series of lesbian encounters – was made in Paris in the spring of 1850.

For a time, the pictures were extremely expensive. In the early 1850s, one daguerreotype cost a week's salary for a French worker. One observer pointed out that it would have been cheaper to hire a prostitute for the day than to buy an image of one. But prices eventually came down and the trade grew exponentially. By 1860, there were estimated to be 400 shops selling pornographic photos in Paris alone. They were available in packs of five on sale from an army of women who kept them under their dresses at all the big train stations. Heterosexual packs normally contained a selection of nude poses, some cunnilingus, some anal sex and some light bondage.

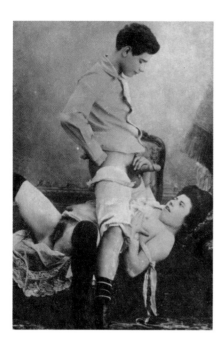

19th-century pornography from Danny Moynihan, *Private Collection: A History of Erotic Photography, 1850–1940.*

Looking at the images now, there can be a basic surprise – a symptom of our egoistic sense of uniqueness – that people could have got up to this sort of thing back then. Our ideas of the past are likely to be so dominated by politics, warfare and the machinations of haughtily attired aristocrats, it can take a moment to remember that our ancestors were far more than this: that there was a lot of cunnilingus and a good deal of anal in the year of the Great Exhibition and the Charge of the Light Brigade.

History teachers may always be attempting to bring the past to life. In a quest for a more intimate sort of history, they sometimes try to show us what houses looked like and what an evening meal might have consisted of. They know how much top hats and cravats can inhibit our powers of empathy. But there is no quicker way to bring the 19th century vividly to our imagination, no more efficient bridge across the centuries, than to be confronted by tangible evidence that our predecessors were, in their deepest selves, despite the gulf in ideology and manners, substantially like us in our more explicit, and most animated, moments. Our peculiar and extreme sexual imaginations – with all the complications and joys these give us – have been thrumming within our species since long before our screens were invented. We can feel at once connected to our ancestors, and less frightened of having lost our innocence at the hands of our new technologies.

There is something else about pornographic photographs with particular relevance to death. Photography's genius lies in its ability to offer us a sense of what feels like the present. It presents a frozen moment of time, rescued from the dissolving force of the years. But this is also what makes photography especially poignant when it is viewed across decades or centuries. We sense with particular clarity the vivacity and immediacy of people in old photos against which one irrevocable fact – that they have all died – stands out with

The past brought
vividly to life.

touching starkness. Their photographic liveliness makes their eventual deaths all the more tangible. Take two people chatting in a street in London in the 1870s. For a moment they live again, and then they – and everything about their world – is washed away in the river of time.

John Thomson,
photograph from *Street Incidents: A Series of Twenty-One Permanent Photographs with Descriptive Letter-Press*, 1881.

The poignancy is even more acute around photographs of children. As they gaze at us, they have so much of a future ahead of them, and yet it is already gone. Everything they were was eventually reduced to nothing.

 Without knowing the details, they grew up, married, became little old ladies and gentlemen and were laid out in their coffins one day.

Such feelings can be heightened around pornography, because having sex is the ultimate activity of the moment, of the fragile bodily self; it is a time when we lose ourselves in the present, absorbed by everything that is contrary to the implacably eternal. The figures in the pornography of the 19th century are our essential contemporaries. They are no different from us – sucking, thrusting, defiling, lost in the emotions of now – and we will eventually go just the way they went.

Yet there is in pornography also a heroic and redemptive defiance of the grim future. In their moment of pleasure, the figures are in glorious denial of what

Children in their Easter best, c. 1910

is going to happen. They don't, right now, care that they will grow old and die – and perhaps they are inviting us not to either. We can watch them holding onto their pleasures and simultaneously cling to our own with new-found gratitude. These people weren't dispirited by their negligible place in the vastness of the cosmos or the implacable progress of the centuries; they had a penis to suck, a vagina to explore, some stockings to put on – and, for a time, they wisely knew how to enjoy their bodies and minds and put aside all thoughts of the upcoming apocalypse.

Image credits

p. 7   MIHAI ANDRITOIU / Alamy Stock Photo

p. 8   Gerard van Honthorst, *The Steadfast Philosopher*, 1623. Oil on canvas,
            151.5 cm × 207.5 cm. Private collection. The Picture Art Collection /
            Alamy Stock Photo

p. 10   Unknown artist, *Origen*, from *Numeros homilia XXVII*, c. 1160. Bayerische
            Staatsbibliothek München, Clm 17092, fol. 130v

p. 11   Unknown miniaturist, *Origen Castrating Himself before a Nun*, 14th century,
            from *Roman de la Rose*, c. 1380. Vellum (parchment) and paint,
            20.5 cm × 14 cm. British Library, London, England

p. 12   Hartmann Schedel, untitled illustration from the *Nuremberg Chronicle*,
            c. 1493. Cambridge University Library, Cambridge, England /
            Wikimedia Commons

p. 13   *The Townley Discobolus*, c. 460–450 BCE. Marble, 169 cm × 105 cm.
            The British Museum, London, England.
            © The Trustees of the British Museum

p. 13   Statues of the Royal Portal, Chartres Cathedral, c. 1145–1245.
            Urban / Wikimedia Commons

p. 14   Medieval gargoyle, Rufford Abbey, c. 1147–1170. leswhalley / Pixabay

p. 16   Tim Graham / Evening Standard / Getty Images

p. 17   Buddha statue, Sukhothai Historical Park, c. 1292–1347. Prasit Rodphan /
            Alamy Stock Photo

p. 25   *Shiva as the Lord of Dance*, made in Tamil Nadu, India, c. 950–1000.
            Sculpture, copper alloy, 76.2 cm × 57.1 cm × 17.7 cm. Los Angeles County
            Museum of Art, LA, USA. Anonymous gift (M.75.1) / Wikimedia Commons

p. 25   William Bouguereau, *The Youth of Bacchus*, 1884. Oil on canvas,
331 cm × 610 cm. Private collection. Sothebys / Wikimedia Commons

p. 28   Everett Collection Inc / Alamy Stock Photo

p. 31   *Virgin and Child in Majesty*, from Auvergne, France, c. 1175–1200.
Wood sculpture, walnut with paint, tin relief on a lead white ground, and
linen, 79.5 cm × 31.7 cm × 29.2 cm. The Metropolitan Museum of Art, New
York, USA. Gift of J. Pierpont Morgan, 1916.

p. 32   Giotto, detail of *Resurrection (Noli me tangere)*, c. 1305. Scrovegni Chapel,
Padua, Italy. Granger Historical Picture Archive / Alamy Stock Photo

p. 33   Michelangelo, *The Creation of Adam*, c. 1508–1512. Fresco, 280 cm × 570 cm.
Sistine Chapel, Vatican, Rome, Italy / Wikimedia Commons

p. 33   Detail from Michelangelo, *The Creation of Adam*, c. 1508–1512. Fresco,
280 cm × 570 cm. Sistine Chapel, Vatican, Rome, Italy. gnuckx / Flickr

p. 34   Edgar Degas, *Study of Hands*, c. 1860. Oil on canvas, 38 cm × 46 cm.
Musée d'Orsay, Paris, France / Wikiart

p. 44   Tom Ferguson / Alamy Stock Photo

p. 55   Geoffrey Robinson / Alamy Stock Photo

p. 58   Leonardo da Vinci, *Studies of the Foetus in the Womb*, c. 1511. Red chalk and
traces of black chalk, pen and ink, wash, 30.4 cm × 22 cm. Royal Collection
Trust, London, England / Wikimedia Commons

p. 63   SNAP / Entertainment Pictures / Alamy Stock Photo

p. 63   Marble statue of Apollo, from Cyrene, Libya, c. 2nd century BCE.
Marble, height: 2.28 m. British Museum, London, England. Jastrow /
Wikimedia Commons

p. 81   themitralvalve.org / Public domain

p. 81   Kevin Gill / Flickr (CC BY 2.0)

p. 83   Eyal Nahmias / Alamy Stock Photo

p. 89   Adam Evans / Wikimedia Commons (CC BY 2.0)

p. 92   Lee Miller, *Picnic (Nusch Eluard, Paul Eluard, Roland Penrose, Man Ray, Ady Fidelin)*, 1937. Gelatin silver print, 203 mm × 197 mm. National Portrait Gallery, London, England. Given by Chris Beetles Fine Photographs, 2013. © Lee Miller Archives, 2020. All rights reserved. leemiller.co.uk

p. 93   *Pablo Picasso with his sister Lola*, 1889. History and Art Collection / Alamy Stock Photo

p. 97   Granger Historical Picture Archive / Alamy Stock Photo

p. 98   Claude Monet, *Poppy Field*, 1873. Oil on canvas, 50 cm × 65 cm. © RMN-Grand Palais (Musée d'Orsay) / Hervé Lewandowski / Wikimedia Commons

p. 99   Peter Stein / Shutterstock

p. 101   Le Corbusier and Jeanneret Pierre, Villa Savoye, Poissy, France, 1928–1931. Paul Kozlowski + © F.L.C. / ADAGP, Paris and DACS, London 2021

p. 101   Le Corbusier and Jeanneret Pierre, Villa Savoye, Poissy, France, 1928–1931. Paul Kozlowski + © F.L.C. / ADAGP, Paris and DACS, London 2021

p. 105   © The British Library

p. 105   Mark Waugh / Alamy Stock Photo

p. 109   Gustave Caillebotte, *Young Man at His Window*, 1875. Oil on canvas, 117 cm × 82 cm. Private collection / Wikimedia Commons

p. 111   Jahnke Bequest, Zurich James Joyce Foundation

p. 120   James Abbott McNeill Whistler, *Anna Whistler*, c. 1850. Alpha Stock / Alamy Stock Photo

p. 120   James Abbott McNeill Whistler, *Arrangement in Grey and Black No. 1*, 1871. Oil on canvas, 144.3 cm × 163 cm. Musée d'Orsay, Paris, France / Wikimedia Commons

p. 122   Joseph Karl Stieler, *Alexander von Humboldt*, 1843. Oil on canvas, 107 cm × 87 cm. Charlottenhof Palace, Potsdam, Germany. Painters / Alamy Stock Photo

p. 123   Roger Eliot Fry, *Clive Bell*, c. 1924. Oil on canvas, 73.4 cm × 60 cm. National Portrait Gallery, London, England. Given by Barbara Bagenal, née Hiles, 1973. © National Portrait Gallery, London

p. 125   John Smart, *A Lady*, 1782. Watercolour on ivory, 5.1 cm × 4.1 cm. Cincinnati Art Museum, Ohio, USA. Acquired from the Collection of T. Everard Spence / Bridgeman Images

p. 127   School of Verona, attributed to Giambettino Cignaroli, *Portrait of Wolfgang Amadeus Mozart at the age of 13 in Verona*, c. 1770. Private Collection. Christie's / Wikimedia Commons

p. 127   Rogier van der Weyden, *Magdalene Reading*, c. 1432. Oil on mahogany, transferred from another panel, 62.2 cm × 54.4 cm. National Gallery, London, England / Wikimedia Commons

p. 127   Giovanni Bellini, detail from *Madonna and the Child between Saints Catherine and Mary Magdalene*, c. 1490. Oil on panel, 58 cm × 107 cm. Gallerie dell'Accademia, Venice, Italy. José Luiz Bernardes Ribeiro / Wikimedia Commons (CC BY-SA 4.0)

p. 128   *Venus of Willendorf*, from Willendorf, Austria, c. 29500 BCE. Limestone, height: 11.1 cm. Naturhistorisches Museum, Vienna, Austria. Thirunavukkarasye-Raveendran / Wikimedia Commons

p. 128   *Aphrodite* or *Crouching Venus*, 2nd century. Marble, 125 cm × 53 cm × 65 cm. British Museum, London, England. Former collection of Sir Peter Lely; lent by H.M. Queen Elizabeth II. Marie-Lan Nguyen / Wikimedia Commons

p. 130   Peter Paul Rubens, *The Three Graces*, 1630–1635. Oil on oak panel, 220.5 cm × 182 cm. Museo del Prado, Madrid, Spain / Wikimedia Commons

p. 131   Ron Burton / Mirrorpix / Getty Images

p. 132   Donald Judd, *15 Untitled Works in Concrete*, 1984. Marfa, Texas, USA. Alpha Stock / Alamy Stock Photo. © Judd Foundation / ARS, NY and DACS, London 2021

p. 142   Pictorial Press Ltd / Alamy Stock Photo

p. 142   Bazmark Films / Warner Bros / Kobal / Shutterstock

p. 149   Gustave Doré, *Death on the Pale Horse*, 1865. Engraving / Wikimedia
          Commons

p. 150   Bernt Notke, detail from *Danse Macabre*, c. 1463–1466. Oil on canvas,
          160 cm × 750 cm. Art Museum of Estonia / Wikimedia Commons

p. 151   Wax vanitas, Europe, c. 1701–1800. Science Museum, London, England.
          Wellcome Collection (CC BY 4.0)

p. 157   eAlisa / Shutterstock

p. 158   J Sharp / Sharp Photography / Wikimedia Commons (CC BY SA 4.0)

p. 158   Dave King / DK / Alamy Stock Photo

p. 161   NaNahara Sung / Shutterstock

p. 162   Pieter Bruegel the Elder, *The Tower of Babel*, 1563. Oil on panel,
          114.4 cm × 155.5 cm. Kunsthistorisches Museum, Vienna, Austria /
          Wikimedia Commons

p. 166   Joaquín Sorolla, *La Siesta*, 1911. Oil on canvas, 300 cm × 300 cm. Sorolla
          Museum, Madrid, Spain / Wikimedia Commons

p. 168   Ansel Adams, *Aspens, Dawn, Autumn, Dolores River Canyon, Colorado*, 1937.
          Gelatin silver print, 23.6 cm × 30.7 cm. © 2020 The Ansel Adams Publishing
          Rights Trust

p. 170   Sueddeutsche Zeitung Photo / Alamy Stock Photo

p. 172   Ary Scheffer, *The Death of Géricault*, 1824. Oil on canvas, 36 cm × 46 cm.
          Musée du Louvre, Paris, France. Web Gallery of Art / Wikimedia Commons

p. 175   John Isaacs, *Are You Still Mad at Me?*, 2001. Courtesy of John Isaacs.

p. 184   Rim of an Attic red-figure kylix, from Athens, Greece, c. 510 BCE.
          Red-figure ceramic, 8.5 cm × 25 cm. Louvre Museum, Paris, France.
          Marie-Lan Nguyen / Wikimedia Commons (CC BY 2.5)

p. 184 Erotic fresco from the House of the Vettii, Pompeii, Italy, 1st century. DeAgostini / Getty Images

p. 184 Peter Fendi, *The Lovers*, 19th century. Public Domain / Wikimedia Commons

p. 185 Félix-Jacques-Antoine Moulin, *Two Standing Female Nudes*, c. 1850. Daguerreotype, 14.5 cm × 11.1 cm. Met Museum, New York. The Rubel Collection, purchase, anonymous gift and Lila Acheson Wallace gift, 1997

p. 186 © Danny Moynihan Collection

p. 188 John Thomson, photograph from *Street Incidents: A Series of Twenty-One Permanent Photographs with Descriptive Letter-Press*, 1881. British Library, Wq4/6069

p. 189 Vintage*Kids / Alamy Stock Photo

The School of Life publishes a range of books on essential topics in psychological and emotional life, including relationships, parenting, friendship, careers and fulfilment. The aim is always to help us to understand ourselves better – and thereby to grow calmer, less confused and more purposeful. Discover our full range of titles, including books for children, here:

www.theschooloflife.com/books

The School of Life also offers a comprehensive therapy service, which complements, and draws upon, our published works:

www.theschooloflife.com/therapy